BRITISH RAILWAYS ILLUSTRATED

Summer Special Number 11

Summer Special No.11

Here Comes Summer...

Welcome to the ELEVENTH British Railways Illustrated SUMMER SPECIAL. All New Photographs and Articles!

Cover photograph. Stanier Pacific 46236 CITY OF BRADFORD, which would have backed out of Euston bound for Camden shed (behind the photographer to the right) on Camden bank in August 1959. The Jubilee on a down train is Longsight's 45631 TANGANYIKA. Prorail UK (Durrant), The Transport Treasury.

Rear cover. Superpower for the Ilfracombe branch. 34002 SALISBURY waits to leave the seaside terminus with the returning Atlantic Coast Express one fine May morning about 1963. In the distance is an incoming train behind another light Pacific. George Heiron.

Frontispiece. A moody NIGHT HAWK at an unknown location – it could well be a corner of Gateshead... E.A. Elias, The Transport Treasury.

Pick up a copy of the monthly magazine BRITISH RAILWAYS ILLUSTRATED at a newsagent, specialist book and model shop or direct from the publisher every month.
Only £3.10

EDITORIAL MATTERS
Contributions, submissions, photographs or whatever (remember the contributor must address and attend to copyright), readers' letters, bouquets and brickbats for British Railways Illustrated must be addressed to Editor,
Chris Hawkins
at 59A, High Street, Clophill, Bedfordshire MK45 4BE
E-mail chris@irwellpress.co.uk
Tel.01525 861888 or
Fax. 01525 862044
Printed & Bound by The Amadeus Press, Bradford, UK
Copyright :- Irwell Press Ltd. 2003

IRWELL PRESS
No.1 in Railway Publishing

The Comedy and the Cauldron Belle Isle

Notes by Tony Wright

A remarkable series of views into the smoking arena of Belle Isle, between the Gas Works Tunnel and Copenhagen Tunnel on the approaches to Kings Cross. It was also the place, it need hardly be added, where one of the best-loved English film comedies was set, *The Ladykillers.* Yet this wonderful sequence is not all, oh no. To celebrate these wondrous photographs and the making of such a well-loved film, a further, DIFFERENT mind-boggling Ladykillers/Belle Isle sequence, with notes once again by Tony Wright, is running now in the *British Railways Illustrated* for July 2003 – don't miss it!

Gateshead's A1 60129 GUY MANNERING leaves the gloom of Copenhagen Tunnel on an Up express in May 1960. In unusually good condition for a Tyneside loco (Geordies always claimed their engines were too often out earning revenue to have time to be cleaned) the light suggests an early train, so she'll probably go back home later in the day. No trains run today through this bore, nor have they for over a quarter of a century. Odd, especially as today, line occupancy is at a premium. Though I haven't visited this location for at least that same length of time, recent pictures of Belle Isle show it horribly overgrown. Such is progress! Photograph Prorail UK (Durrant)/The Transport Treasury.

i'll Remember those Black and White Days...

Near to the end of steam into King's Cross, 60061 PRETTY POLLY leaves the access road from Top Shed (beyond and through the arches to the right) ready to run back to pick up its express. The signal is just returning to 'on'. She's a dear old lady, by now in final condition; double chimney, German blinkers, divided handrail on smoke box door and numberplate on top hingestrap (even though both sixes are still incorrect). As a professional model maker I urge others of similar lunacy to look at this racehorse's (parrot's?) dome and finally put to bed the notion of 'banjo' as a description of latter-day A3s and other Pacific domes. It is streamlined in shape and needs describing as such. The 'banjo' domes were only fitted to the 1934-built A3s, and then probably lasted only up to their first boiler change. The train on the Down Fast is probably an outer suburban diagram for the carriages are non-gangwayed BR Mk1s. It's on its way to Hitchin or beyond, perhaps even Peterborough and is probably diesel-hauled by this date. The coach next to the engine rejoices in the title of semi-corridor lavatory composite and replicates a design by both Gresley and Thompson, unique (I think) to the ER. Shortly afterwards, PRETTY POLLY ascends the bank on the Down Fast. Photographs Prorail UK (Durrant)/ The Transport Treasury.

You'll Remember those Black and White Days...

Another late steam shot sees 60148 ABOYEUR awaiting the signal to gain access to the road ready to reverse back to pick up its train, though it will have to wait for the train signalled on the Down Slow to pass first. Just behind, an A4 is nosing up close to the A1's tender, after leaving Top Shed in its turn. Photograph Prorail UK (Durrant)/The Transport Treasury.

Left. The photographer has now moved along to the western side of the cutting, putting both Pacifics in the sunlight. The A4 behind ABOYEUR is now revealed as 60021 WILD SWAN (a curious choice of name, given that few swans are truly tame – surely Mute Swan would have been better?). Both locos will run down eventually to the terminus together to pick up their respective trains, thus saving a path at busy times and it can be noted that they didn't couple together in the shed yard but only at the last moment, once in the Belle Isle cauldron, close to the signal box from where, presumably, the instructions were issued. Double heading would never have been contemplated – on the GN, never Sir, despite what happened regularly next door or just up the road. Even in June 1963, just before the end of official steam into King's Cross, many of the trains had Gresley, Thompson or Peppercorn Pacifics. If ever a Region bowed to dieselisation with its steam reputation still intact it was the Eastern. It's not clear what the chap on the running plate is doing; probably he's the Fireman off WILD SWAN, settling some final procedural matter or merely passing the last few moments before the 'off'. Photograph Prorail UK (Durrant)/The Transport Treasury.

Above. WILD SWAN now gets away with a stopping passenger train (note single, central headlamp) probably going as far as Peterborough. The use of Pacifics on these trains was not just confined to the end of steam, though a Top Shed A4 would have been unlikely much earlier. New England had a stud of Thompson A2s and one Peppercorn A2; they were used on these tightly timed trains, though the stock was not always top rate gangwayed Mk1s as illustrated here. 60021 was one of 34A's remaining A4s which migrated to New England briefly on the closure of its long time home, though it didn't last long enough to eventually go to Scotland. Photograph Prorail UK (Durrant)/ The Transport Treasury.

With the shadows slightly longer, ABOYEUR now gets away, this time on a fully fitted freight. It's on the Down Slow (relief) and appears to have originated from the passenger station or alongside it. Was this unusual? Most shots of freights leaving Kings Cross, express or otherwise, show them leaving from the goods yard (the upper roads to the right of this picture). I don't think 60148 is on a parcels train for the stock beneath her smoke is all four-wheeled vans. Photograph Prorail UK (Durrant)/The Transport Treasury.

An unknown, but gloriously-lit and torpedo-like A4 powers its way north towards the end of steam in 1963. It has a long nameplate and tows the correct style streamlined non-corridor tender; 60003 ANDREW K. McCOSH was withdrawn at the end of 1962 so my guess is that it's 60008 DWIGHT D. EISENHOWER. By this date, as expected, most of this express is made up of Mk1 stock, though the first coach is a Thompson brake. The fifth coach too is pre-nationalisation, judging by the central row of ventilators. Photograph Prorail UK (Durrant)/The Transport Treasury.

This time it's definitely 60008 IKE, on another day but with identical stock. A double-chimney V2 is just getting clearance to run down to the terminus for its train. Photograph Prorail UK (Durrant)/The Transport Treasury.

In May 1960 one of Hornsey's ubiquitous J50s takes empty stock out to the suburbs for servicing. These were sturdy, powerful tanks and judging by the steam to spare at the safety valves this heavy job is well within its limits. That same steam has annoyingly obscured the loco arriving in the background, and all we can glimpse is its tender, telling us it's a B1, K3 or V2. The first coach in the ECS set appears to be a later built (note angle trussing) Gresley Brake Third (later Second) Open. Photograph Prorail UK (Durrant)/The Transport Treasury.

Left. One of Top Shed's celebrated A3s, 60062 MINORU on the Up Fast, soon to pass through the eastern bore of Gasworks Tunnel, in May 1960. It will end up in one of the lower-numbered platforms at the terminus, though obviously not the first one, for the parallel Cravens unit will have to go somewhere. The A3 looks in beautiful nick and apart from the acquisition of German blinkers and a speedo is just about in final condition, with double chimney and AWS fitted. If one were making a model of her, would one incorporate the slightly bent handrail, not parallel to the ejector pipe? The Sheffield-built DMUs were a common sight for many years at the 'Cross, working on suburban services, something they were never designed for. Two car sets were typical on services throughout the day, outside the rush hours. Branch lines should have been their destiny, though someone seems to have forgotten that these were being closed as fast as the units were being built. Photograph Prorail UK (Durrant)/The Transport Treasury.

Below. MALLARD climbs past Belle Isle with the Down Flying Scotsman in May 1960. Earlier, the Talisman would have set off for the same destination, Edinburgh Waverley, though we'll have to wait another month before the third train of the 'set', the non-stop Elizabethan, will be running as well, at the start of that year's summer timetable. MALLARD, one of the A4s which indulged in much tender swopping, has a 1928 corridor sort in tow, though it's not the cut-down one she had twelve years previously – that's gone to 60029 WOODCOCK. Not long prior to May 1960 she had a 1935 corridor tender, the type she'll get next and keep to preservation in April 1963 – when she'll end up with a streamlined non-corridor type. Photograph Prorail UK (Durrant)/The Transport Treasury.

A Cleethorpes-King's Cross express slows under adverse distants for eventual entry to the terminus, in front of the North London Viaduct, in 1963. It's impossible to identify the Britannia Pacific – the name's a short one, so it could be BOADICEA. These trains had become the responsibility of a small stud of Britannias after they lost their top link GE work and how well they did on them. They must still have been considered slightly secondary duties though, judging by the first two cars in the set, which are Thompson vehicles. Photograph Prorail UK (Durrant)/The Transport Treasury.

Almost at the end of main line GN steam power, 60108 GAY CRUSADER is still considered good enough to have charge of a northbound express, which appears to be made up of BR Mk1s. Such a degrading condition for a top link loco was fortunately not universal on the main line at this time, as other pictures in this series will show. However, for GAY CRUSADER (today she might be called 'Same Gender Orientation Person on a Mission) no more cleaning would ever take place and on her last journey from Grantham she looked, sadly, just like this. Photograph Prorail UK (Durrant)/The Transport Treasury.

A truly fascinating shot taken towards the end of GN main line steam, in 1963. Stock for the Tees Tyne Pullman awaits entry into the terminus, soon to be heading northwards. It's the Tees Tyne because the nearest wholly visible car is the Hadrian Bar, unique to this train. The light direction also suggests it's too late to be the service Up train and the motive power, a Brush Type 2, confirms it. It is tempting to think that the A4 waiting in the shed access/exit road is to power the Pullman but I don't think so. A couple of years before, maybe, but by now the Pullman passengers will fly north behind another type which gained an ECML pedigree, a Deltic. Serene above the lot is a Fairburn 2-6-4T – one of the crew appears to have got out for a really good view. Photograph Prorail UK (Durrant)/The Transport Treasury.

Locally based A4 60015 QUICKSILVER performs the familiar movement of crossing from the Up Fast to pass through the centre bore of Gasworks Tunnel in August 1959. The North London Viaduct crosses in the background with Copenhagen Tunnel lost beyond. This picture is of note because it shows QUICKSILVER during the very short time when it didn't tow its original style corridor tender. Here she's got a 1928 corridor sort. Only SILVER FOX of her immediate silver sisters retained the 1935 style throughout its life – the other two changing theirs at various times. The visible stock in the train is truly representative of the period with Thompson, Gresley and Mk1 vehicles all in the set. On the engine line, an A3 waits to follow to pick up its train. Photograph Prorail UK (Durrant)/The Transport Treasury.

One of New England's usually grubby V2s, 60912, heads a Down express in September 1959 – view is from the top of Copenhagen Tunnel. It's probably a secondary service (no catering vehicles) made up of an almost equal mix of Gresleys and Mk1s. It might only be going as far as Peterborough itself. The Up distants with their low arms (in order to be seen as the trains leave Copenhagen Tunnel) are, left to right, Up Slow (relief) straight on, Up Slow to Up Fast, Up Fast straight on and Up Fast to centre bore of Gasworks tunnel. Photograph Prorail UK (Durrant)/The Transport Treasury.

A Doncaster V2, quite a bit cleaner than 60912, prepares for the plunge into Gasworks tunnel centre bore (out of sight to left) with an Up relief express, possibly a summer Saturday extra, about 1960. This V2 has had its original monoblock cylinder casting replaced by three separate ones, characterised by the hefty outside steampipes. Photograph Prorail UK (Durrant)/The Transport Treasury.

Filming *The Ladykillers*: 1. The film crew had two V2s put at their disposal, 60821 and 60814. The latter is clumping south wrong line on the Goods Lines out of Copenhagen Tunnel with a train of empties (ready for falling bodies!) on 3 July 1955. Each V2 had its own train of empty minerals, kept out of the way in Kings Cross Goods Yard during the week as filming took place over six successive Sundays in 1955. Care had to be taken that they were not sent away north in the meantime, ruining the continuity! The V2s, despite the crews' best efforts, did not make enough smoke and the 'special effects' men, as we can see, pumped out some more. Photograph P.J. Kelley.

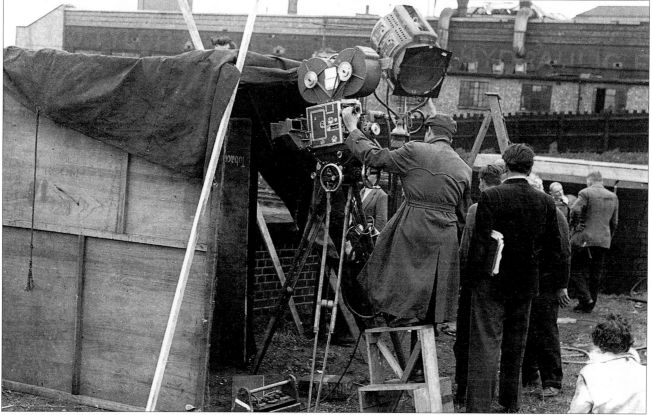

Filming *The Ladykillers*: 2. The crew in action above Copenhagen Tunnel, 3 July 1955; the Director, Alex Mackendrick, is the chap with the papers under his arm. The place for the filming (was there ever a more memorable one?) was arranged by the ER Publicity people – something probably impossible in these over-regulated times. Photograph P.J. Kelley.

Western 2-10-0s

The last 9F, 92220 EVENING STAR, at Old Oak Common shed in September 1962; it was based in London briefly (for a few weeks only) around this time, going before the end of the year to Oxford. Since its last notable visit to Old Oak, in April 1960, a few weeks after construction (see BRILL Vol.11 No.3, December 2001) it had had mainly been at Canton. There were spells at Bath Green Park either side of its stay in the London Division but it returned to South Wales, at East Dock, for the last year or so of its all-too brief BR life. Photograph Prorail UK (Durrant), The Transport Treasury.

The first 9F and the first on the Western Region, 92000 at Ebbw Junction shed on April 1961. The first eight 9Fs, 92000-92007, had gone new to Ebbw Junction at the beginning of 1954. They had not been well received and spent much of that year out of use consequent upon regulator and brake problems but once this mini-fleet got going the Ebbw Junction 9Fs (though admittedly with relatively low mileages due to the nature of the duties) put in an availability record of 87%, the highest of any BR Standard on any Region. Photograph Prorail UK (Durrant), The Transport Treasury.

You'll Remember those Black and White Days...

And one in the middle. 92217, built in 1959 and at first a Canton engine, is on Sapperton bank in 1964, by which time it had gone to Tyseley, just in time to become an LMR 9F. Photograph Prorail UK (Durrant), The Transport Treasury.

HOTSPUR at Home

Britannia Pacific 70011 HOTSPUR spent the first ten years of its life as a Norwich engine, pounding up to Liverpool Street and back on the revolutionised GE services. Like several others, it then had a sort of twilight existence at March (where a number of the Pacifics even went into store for a period) from September 1961 to December 1963 before going, like all the rest, to the London Midland Region. It never spent time on the GN Grimsby services, working out of Immingham, like other GE Britannias and once it got to the LM stayed at Carlisle, either Kingmoor or Upperby, until withdrawal at the end of 1967. Here it is at home at March about 1962, hidden amid the drifting smoke and the ranks of 8Fs and other engines. The building was the five road 'servicing shed' erected when the LNER rearranged and modernised the whole place (the work included the coaling plant) over the late 1920s-early 1930s. Photographs The Transport Treasury

You'll Remember those Black and White Days...

RT ... WAR REPORT ... WAR REPO

FIGHTING THE FIRES

Practice and the real thing on the Southern and the Great Western. Blackfriars Goods continues to burn on 16 November 1940 as a hose is played over the interior. The work of fire fighting depended of course on long and intensive training and exercise, which had been underway since at least the Munich Crisis of 1938. On a sunny day in 1939 the Paddington Auxiliary Brigade was training at the Royal Oak end of Paddington Goods Depot. The island canopy of Royal Oak station is in the background; Ranelagh Bridge engine yard lies behind the box vans. Note the perfect turnout of the blokes; tin hats, gas masks and, in a couple of cases, civvy trousers. Desperate times were ahead...

The End is Nigh...
Nine Elms

The way in which BR chose to run down its dwindling steam fleet must remain a thing of unutterable regret. It was as if, at some point in the early 1960s, steam was deemed beyond the pale; it became clear that career development, for anyone with half an eye on advancement, lay in distancing yourself from steam operation. The further the distance, the better. There would be no money for steam, not even the minimum, it seemed at times, to keep it staggering on. The once mighty Nine Elms bore sad witness to much of this; take 34090 (SIR EUSTACE MISSENDEN SOUTHERN RAILWAY) on the outdoor washing out roads (outdoors since the Germans bombed the shed) bereft of nameplates and covered in grime. The fitter in his wellies looks to be attending the injectors, blissfully unaware that if the health and safety deluge of today had taken form back in the 1960s then his job would have gone even sooner. Photograph The Transport Treasury.

You'll Remember those Black and White Days...

Nine Elms was huge, surely one of the biggest in the country and despite its annexation by the present fruit and veg market, the vast site is still strikingly clear on any map of London. It had taken many years to get a great shed to this neglected, part-ruinous state. An absurd race had developed, first to be the 'first' Region to rid itself of steam and then to be ahead of other big countries in Western Europe. We saw water columns taken out of service while steam locomotives were still turning up from *foreign* Regions. Worse, sheds closed in a similarly precipitate way to please accountants and thereby show 'savings'. Increasingly decrepit, they trundled miles for servicing. Another wheeze was to halt the provision of spares, with sheds expected to cannibalise engines to keep others going. The most distressing aspect, to observers, was the abandonment of the most rudimentary cleaning. Recruitment difficulties were of course immense and cleaners as a species largely disappeared yet it was not just that. There was the petty (as the late great Peter Winding called it) decision to stop the supply of cotton waste for cleaning. He wrote that the great contrast was France, where steam remained on a par with the newer forms of traction till the end, properly maintained and operated. This picture certainly catches *la différence*... Photograph The Transport Treasury.

As the end approached the wide expanse of yard, occupied by far fewer engines, only served to accentuate the dereliction. Just look at the wasteland of clinker, ash and spilt coal, a battered corrugated iron sheet and a single dilapidated light Pacific on the ash roads, where once there had been queues. In the background, across the SW main line, rises up Nine Elms Gas Works. The light Pacific may be neglected but it is certainly not shy of steam – just marvel at the escape from the safety valves, roaring up into the sky and setting one pigeon at least to flight. Photograph The Transport Treasury.

Conversations at the front of the 'New Shed'. Photograph The Transport Treasury.

The engine roads of the 'Old Shed', ruined in the Second World War and afterwards used simply as open or partly open roads for storing dead engines, washouts and other maintenance. 35003 has usefully had its number chalked on the buffer beam – doubtless its ROYAL MAIL plates have been removed. It is in steam, despite the 'NOT TO BE MOVED' plate. The picture is remarkable too for the pouring chimneys of Battersea Power Station, throbbing away in the background by the banks of the Thames. Photograph The Transport Treasury.

You'll Remember those Black and White Days...

Everyday scenes at Nine Elms in the last year or so. Note how so little has changed, with the lads manhandling a connecting rod across the pits of the 'Old Shed' into the relatively luxurious confines of the 'New Shed'; at least it had a roof. Outside the once crowded yard was, as was usual by this time, largely uninhabited. It was sad and dismal but while we all rued the final demise of Nine Elms in 1967 there was a group who profoundly did not – the long-suffering inhabitants of those flats! Photographs The Transport Treasury.

Last Day at Middleton

You'll Remember those Black and White Days...

The last day rites on the Cromford and High Peak brought crowds to Middleton Top and the various sections of the otherwise lonely and desolate line. Of the two J94 0-6-0STs, 68006 and 68012, the latter somehow managed to acquire a York 50A shedplate at some point in the day (compare the pictures – now you see it now you don't...). The devotees were at least blessed with decent weather on Sunday 30 April 1967. Certainly few of them were dressed for the High Peak if it chose one of its less benign moods! And just look at the state of the poor old Middleton shed. One of the few in the *Shed Directory* with its position given in degrees of longitude and latitude, it unfortunately did not survive with the now preserved engine house. It is not hard to see why... Photographs The Transport Treasury.

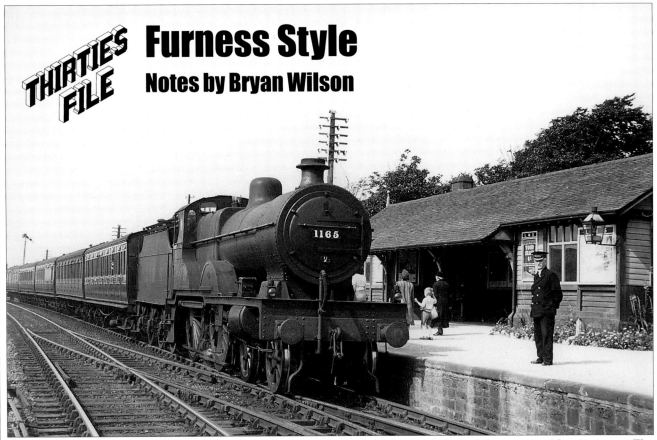

THIRTIES FILE

Furness Style
Notes by Bryan Wilson

Ravenglass with an up express running in. Express it may be but the stock is mainly non-corridor it seems. The Station Master in his best hat is watching what the photographer is up to. The poster board behind him invites you to reserve a seat for a shilling. Carnforth had half a dozen Compounds in the 1930s, mainly for the Ulster boat trains for which they were responsible between Morecambe and Crewe. They obviously wandered up the coast as well. Photograph I. Clarke, The Transport Treasury.

Former L&Y 2-4-2T 10643 stands in Ulverston station with the Lakeside branch train. This was the third Ulverston station, dating from 1874 with its clock tower (just visible) which incorporated 'corner urns', all the work of architects Paley & Austin of Lancaster. The adverts are for Veno's cough cure and the Railway Passengers Assurance Company. As for 10643 itself, it went to Plodder Lane when the Lakeside service was suspended during the Second World War but came back for a couple of years afterwards. It is motor fitted and carries a short bunker. It lasted until October 1958. Its 'home shed' at the time of the photograph, Lakeside itself, closed on 3 February 1947. Photograph I. Clarke, The Transport Treasury.

You'll Remember those Black and White Days...

Bowness Pier joined Ambleside in being a Furness Railway station without tracks. The steamers serving it were effectively an extension of the Ulverston-Lakeside branch line. An 1866 Act allowed the Furness Railway to invest in the Windermere United Steam Yacht Company, which they purchased in 1875. The style of Furness building is familiar; note the 'London, Midland & Scottish Railway' billboards, not to mention the bath chair. Photograph I. Clarke, The Transport Treasury.

Only some eighteen months old, Stanier 2-6-4T 42595, new to Barrow in November 1936, stands in the down platform at Ravenglass adjacent to the Furness goods shed. Sharp eyes will note that the telegraph pole on the up side is secured by strap to the shed, an indication of what winter can be like here when the 'westerlies' start to blow. A nice Furness signal completes the scene. Photograph I. Clarke, The Transport Treasury.

Treherbert and Beyond
A South Wales Engine Shed Tale
Bryan Wilson

The Taff Vale Railway

Railway penetration of the Rhondda began in June 1841 when the linking of the Dinas Tramroad to the Taff Vale Railway at 'Aerw' was completed. (Dinas Colliery had been mentioned as a 'sale coal' undertaking in Brunel's Report of February 1835). There was some urgency in pushing further up the Valley as in 1845 a rival company, the broad gauge 'Rhondda and Ely Valleys Junction Railway', was incorporated to run from Blaenrhondda through Penygraig to Lanelay Bridge near Llantrisant and link up with the South Wales main line. The Taff Vale Railway therefore presented its own Bill to Parliament to extend the Pontypridd-Eirw branch not merely to Dinas, but all the way to the top of the Rhondda Fawr at Tynewydd, with a branch up the Rhondda Fach to Ffaldau. Royal Assent was received on 26 August 1846 although at that time the full extent of the Rhondda coalfield was uncertain. By September 1850,

however, work on Lord Bute's trial pit at Cwmsaerbren (Treherbert) had started.

The Rhondda Fawr branch reached Dinas by May 1849, Gelligaled (Ystrad) by December 1855, and Bute Merthyr Colliery at Treherbert on 7 August 1856. This showed considerable foresight by the Taff Vale Company as the presence of steam coal in the upper Rhondda Fawr was not proved until 1853. The first load of coal from Cwmsaerbren Colliery came out on 21 December 1855 and was carted to Ystrad to go by rail from there. Though the Taff Vale itself reached Treherbert Bute Merthyr Colliery in August 1856 it was 12 January 1863 before passenger services commenced, the TVR having acquired land from Lord Bute for a station at 'Cwmsaerbren' in 1861. It should be pointed out that Tref Herbert ('Herbert's town', possibly named after the landowner Herbert de Winton) was first mentioned in the Parish Records in March 1855, but Cwmsaerbren

appears in the records as the location until Treherbert passenger station opened.

Eight months after the passenger service commenced in 1864 a large building 'used as an engine and carriage house' at Treherbert burned down. It was nearly a year later before reconstruction was authorised and a semi-roundhouse, made of blue pennant stone from Craig yr Hesg quarry at Pontypridd, was erected in 1866. The Taff Vale also built a row of houses on the down side between the station and the site of the 1931 engine shed. They still stand, in good order.

Rhondda & Swansea Bay Railway

When speculators surveyed the Rhondda coalfield, Swansea was obviously regarded as a possible outlet but at the time the Swansea 'City Fathers' were not ambitious and forward-looking enough (compare with TVR outlook above) to support a scheme. It was not until the 1880s that things began to

Left. The complete building, being fitted out in February 1931. It is a replica of the 1929 rebuilt Abercynon, but twice the size. 'Stephenson Clarke' private owner wagons are in use for inwards material as well as 'NE' and 'LMS'. Modellers should note the position of the private owner wagon numbers on the end boards, together with the tare weight. This was typical 'Stephenson Clarke' practice.

Below. The Government Loans & Guarantees Act in action, and a view repaying careful study. It is 27 February 1931 and work is underway. The shed is the building right of centre and appears to be complete, as is the coal stage apart from its elevated water tank. A gang of men are engaged on trackwork. To raise the site to the height shown, a temporary 2ft gauge railway was provided for Messrs. Jordan's to access Ynysfeio Colliery for waste material. This involved making a temporary bridge across the Rhondda River and utilised two four-wheeled petrol mechanical locos. One track of this railway enters the shed yard, the other runs left towards the main line signals where some narrow gauge wagons can be seen just in front of the box van. The river bridge crossing was not perpetuated after construction of the shed and yard was complete. The colliery on the left is Bute Merthyr and the new signal box in the middle (the Rhondda Valleys Brewery stands behind it) is Treberbert South, which replaced 'Bute Merthyr Colliery' just out of view to the left. As can be seen, despite the 1927 Report, the carriage sidings are clearly on the up side, opposite the box.

happen. At that time, it should be remembered, it was a long circuitous journey by rail via Pontypridd, Cardiff and the main line from the top of the Rhondda to Swansea Docks. Including the congestion in the Rhondda Valley, it could take up to a week!

By this time, the Rhondda wanted to rid itself of the Taff Vale monopoly and Swansea likewise wanted to be free of the GWR one. This concentrated minds. An 1880 Bill originally attempted to connect the Rhondda with Port Talbot but it was the act of 10 August 1882 which stipulated that the Rhondda starting point for the new 'Rhondda & Swansea Bay Railway' would be fixed at Treherbert. The R&SB was not a combined Dock and Railway Company like many of the others although it made sure, of course, that it had the backing of the Swansea Harbour authorities regarding Rhondda steam coal.

The first portion of the line from Aberavon to Pontrhydyfen was opened on 25 June 1885 and in November of that year had reached Cymmer. Running powers were provided over the GWR from Aberavon (Port Talbot) into Swansea but this did not break the GW monopoly. There was even a proposal for a tunnel under the River Neath to avoid the GWR and reach Swansea but after the inevitable protest from the 'shipping fraternity', they settled for a river bridge below Neath and an Act in 1891 for the new Railway from Aberavon to Briton Ferry and Danygraig, reaching there in March 1895.

At the north end, the line reached Blaengwynfi in June 1890 and passed through the 3,443 yard

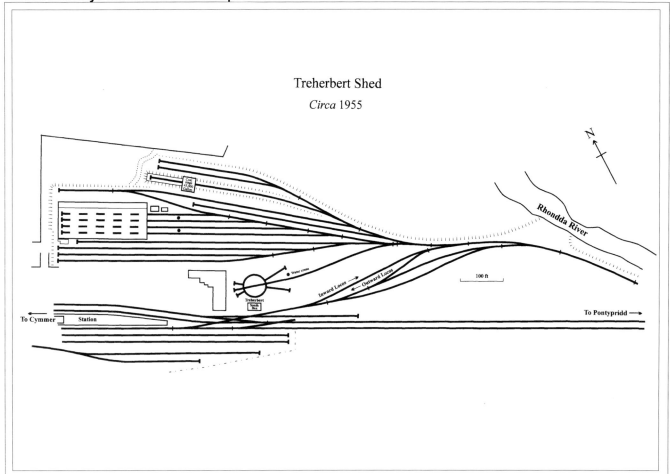

Treherbert Shed

Circa 1955

Rhondda Tunnel (3rd longest in Wales if you include the Severn Tunnel, taking five years to build) to Blaenrhondda a month later. It was 14 July 1890 that the Treherbert objective was achieved. Inevitably, there were nearly three years of discussion (and sometimes argument) before the TVR and R&SB sorted themselves out at the station. The TVR objected to joint ownership and the boundary between the two companies eventually settled at a junction (with the TVR's Fernhill Colliery extension) twenty chains north of the station. The single platform on the down side at Treherbert became an island in 1901 and remained in this form until 1972.

The Sheds
The first engine shed at Treherbert opened in 1864 and enjoyed only a short life, as noted earlier. The second shed, on the up side of the station, opened in 1866, a curious arrangement of seven roads in 'semi-roundhouse' fashion, like St Blazey, plus three 'open' roads. The original Taff Vale intention had been to erect facilities at Ystrad for the working of coal trains down the valley, but Treherbert became the preferred location.

By 1927, thoughts were turning to a replacement for the 1866 shed. As early as 27 January that year the Loco, Carriage and Stores

Committee recorded that '1 Acre, 0 Rod and 1 Perch' of land had been acquired 'for reproduction of carriage sidings to be displaced by the proposed Locomotive Depot'. This was merely an accounting device as the site in mind was, as several photographs prove, on completely open land. The carriage siding 'reproduction' actually consisted of two new ones and the extension of three existing ones on the up side. The work was carried out around July 1928.

On 10 October 1929, the Committee examined the 'Provision of a new Engine Shed and Improved Coal and Watering facilities' at Treherbert, recording the estimates as £48,750 for the shed and £2,750 for land. In February 1930 the contract, 'at a sum not to exceed £44,000', was let to Jordan's of Newport, Monmouthshire, a firm which also constructed the exactly similar buildings at Radyr and Pantyffynnon.

By May 1930 the Great Western had applied for Government money under the Loans and Guarantees Act (designed to create work in the Depression); by now the estimate for Treherbert shed was confirmed as £48,750. The four road building in the aptly termed 'Loan Act Style' duly appeared on the down side, slightly south of the station. The style was quite distinct and happily one survives to this day – the GWS

HQ at Didcot. Treherbert itself survived until the end of steam, in March 1965.

The R&SB kept its own locomotive at Blaenrhondda, a site actually at the end of Gwendoline Street, Tynewydd, nearer to Treherbert, from 1891. This was probably a temporary arrangement, for a replacement shed was provided in 1894. It was blown down in December 1914. It latterly housed one 2-4-2T and though locomotives 'lived' there until August 1922, local intelligence suggests they went to Treherbert shed for other than the simplest of attention.

The Engines
Treherbert had an outstation shed at Ferndale; the allocations at the two inevitably became 'mixed' but some engines did manage a fair spell of time with one or other shed over the years. At the start of 1926, a total of 37 locos were allocated of which Taff Vale O1 No.473 and 'Dean Goods' 2434 and 2470 were known to be at Ferndale. Interesting residents at this time were two of the 39XX tanks, rebuilt from Dean Goods, Nos.3908 and 3913 which worked Treherbert to Swansea Riverside passenger trains. Otherwise it was a mix of Taff Vale 0-6-2Ts, 56XXs and the three incline locos Nos.792, 793 and 794 for Pwllyrhebog. Through the years, there was always one loco at

You'll Remember those Black and White Days...

On 27 February 1931 the yard is partially complete, though with most of the PW men out of the way. The shed itself is already overshadowing the surrounding terraced houses.

Treherbert fitted with the 'haulage attachment' for this incline, in addition to the nominated locos. In 1926, it was No.552 (Old Taff Vale No.151) of the M1 class.

By 1934, the engines numbered 42, of which 12 were outbased at Ferndale (where the shed hailed from 1884, replacing one of 1866 vintage). Inevitably, no less than 25

of the popular 56XXs were allocated, but there was now a novelty in No.152 (old Cardiff Railway No.22). The 'haulage' or 'incline' standby was Taff Vale N No.486 which took over

By 9 October 1931 the shed was 'in business'. We have a pristine coaling stage and water tank with tracks and pit (almost) immaculate. The staple diet of 0-6-2Ts is in place though, arguably, more interesting is the PW bogie vehicle 40630 against the buffer stops. Its livery is all-over black with white lettering. The locally named 'Table Mountain' rises above the shed.

An excellent view of the completed shed yard with 5636 prominent, having enjoyed the 'oily' clean at which South Wales so excelled. The loco was only six years old at the time. A fine Departmental coach stands alongside the shed. As was the custom in the South Wales valleys, the 'brake van road' is adjacent to the shed, in this case on the left. The brake went with the loco at the start of the day's work and they were seldom parted.

The coal stage and the north end of the new turntable (of distinctive GW design) and more Stephenson Clarke wagons.

from No.552 in July 1930. By this time, the 39XXs had gone, as had the Dean Goods. Throughout the 1930s, there was a slight trend back towards 'Taff' tanks from the GW 56XXs; there were sixteen of the 'Taffs' resident in January 1938. Despite the number of 56XX tanks that spent much of their lives at Treherbert and Ferndale, not one spent its whole life there. No.5674 came nearest, starting and finishing its life at the shed but with a spell away in the middle.

In May 1935, 0-6-0T No.2750 gained the 'haulage attachment' from No.486. This loco was a bit different in that it stayed allocated to Merthyr, where there were others of its class. There it remained 'officially' until 1945 when, in turn, it was replaced by pannier tank No.7722, which was properly allocated to Treherbert.

At Nationalisation, the 'Taff' contingent of tanks had risen to nineteen and 2-6-2T No.5159 was on the books. Two more of these, Nos.4162 and 4177, had arrived by June 1950 plus the first two 66XXs, Nos.6648 and 6655. The Pwllyrhebog Incline closed in July 1951 and the three 0-6-0s, Nos.193, 194 and 195, were stored at Treherbert but they

all had an 'afterlife', albeit short, at places like the NCB Treorchy and the Tar Distillation Plant at Caerphilly.

When the Cardiff Valleys Interval Service started in 1952, Treherbert lost seven locomotives and in February 1954 the complement was down to 28 including only half a dozen at Ferndale. Of interest by then was BR Standard 3MT 2-6-2T No.82000 and five 84XX panniers which found some work, which is more than some of their brethren did, at Ferndale. The three GW 2-6-2Ts at this time were Nos.5159, 5162 and 5195. From now on, it was mostly downhill with retraction, closures of collieries and sidings until the shed ceased to function in March 1965, having outlived Ferndale by six months.

The Men and their Work
There was a fair mix of passenger and mineral work at Treherbert. The passenger jobs took them to Cardiff and Barry Island and to Swansea (East Dock, Riverside and High Street over the years). Sunday School and seaside trips took them to Aberavon and Porthcawl, the latter via Tonteg and Llantrisant which was the route taken by the wartime Workmen's trains to

Tremains. These ran out and back for all three shifts when the factory was at its peak.

When the Steel Company of Wales was developing Abbey Works at Port Talbot, there were Workmen's trains from Porth to Port Talbot via Aberavon and the R&SB/GW connection to the South Wales main line. On coal trains, Treherbert men worked to Barry Docks (or Cadoxton), Roath Branch and Radyr Sidings, also to Bassaleg and Newport Docks via the Pontypridd Caerphilly and Newport/AD&R route (indeed the purpose of the Pontypridd Caerphilly and Newport was to move coal from the Rhondda and Aberdare Valleys to Newport Docks). There were also workings to Merthyr and Aberdare via the triangle at Pontypridd and to Penarth Docks via Radyr Quarry as well as Swansea Docks via the R&SB. It was all quite a mix. In the 1950s, apart from all these 'through' journeys, there were seventeen 'target' jobs, which shunted everywhere and anywhere.

In the 1950s there were 31 turns in the Treherbert Goods Link and 28 in the Passenger. Additionally, there was a treble shifted pilot at the shed, the 'Shed Link' (one set

on the two day turns and two sets on nights) for preparation and disposal of engines and the shed shunting. The night shift staff were also used as 'knockers up' for those who needed raising from bed before day came. There were also men out-based at Pwllyrhebog until the incline closed.

There were trips to Fernhill Colliery, banking duties at Blaenycwm, shunting at Trealaw, Treorchy and Cwmparc. One of the afternoon trips (TP6) was a bit different in that it worked the pick up goods at 1.40pm Treherbert to Tonypandy and returned up the valley with coal, either for domestic sale, or for forwarding down the R&SB. Quantities of coal passing down the R&SB from Treherbert never matched the Taff Vale route, as the price of steam coal in earlier years at Cardiff, Barry and Newport was usually 4d or 6d a ton above the that for the same coal at Swansea. Colliery owners naturally wanted the highest price. Additionally, the gradient was in favour of the load.

To get to Swansea via the R&SB meant taking traffic up the hill to the Rhondda Tunnel only for it to go down again. Banking was also necessary from Treherbert up to

Blaenrhondda Colliery at the top of the Rhonnda Valley. On the Swansea services, the Automatic Train Control (ATC) had to be operative for the Briton Ferry-Swansea High Street main line section and only some of the 0-6-2Ts had it. These, principally, were the 66XX and notably No.6648 (although 5608, 5636, 5680 and 5695 were later involved). Landore and Neath sheds also had duties over the line, Neath occasionally sending one of the rare breed of 81XX 2-6-2Ts, No.8104.

The 8.20pm Treherbert-Swansea returned from that city with fish and milk (in churns) from west Wales and arrived back at about 3.0am. The train continued down the Taff to Pontypridd before returning light to shed. This through engine working, from the R&SB to the Taff line, was unusual, as most through trains changed locos at Treherbert. Over the years, such services had a variety of starting and terminating points including Bute Road, Penarth and Cadoxton one end and Briton Ferry, Neath and Swansea at the other.

Ferndale Outpost

Locomotives out-stationed here returned to Treherbert for boiler

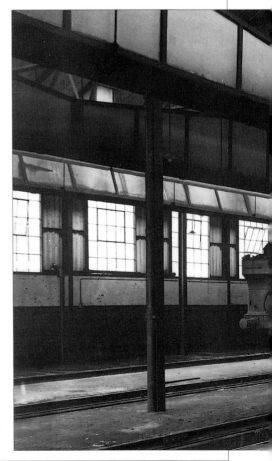

You'll Remember those Black and White Days...

Left. Looking north to the back of the shed, 9 October 1931. One of the Pwllyrhebog Incline locos is at the back of No.4 road, otherwise 0-6-2Ts rule. The shed is in pristine condition, light and airy with clean pits.

Below. A Pwllyrhebog Incline loco is on the stops of No.4 road (right) on 15 December 1931 with two 56XX 0-6-2Ts booked for passenger work on 'TB' and 'TC' turns. Note locos facing either way, depending on whether their next job was towards Swansea or Cardiff. Apart from keeping the firebox covered when working uphill, it was desirable to have the pony wheels leading for the faster downhill speeds, to at least 'guide' the engine somewhat round curves and through pointwork.

washing, piston and valve exams and attention to side rods. Coaling at Ferndale was by crane and bucket. The Treherbert foreman visited Ferndale three times a week as part of his supervisory duties.

Incidents

One of the Workmen's trains from Treherbert was the 5.47am to Duffryn Rhondda Platform on the R&SB, via the Rhondda Tunnel. The train consisted of five vehicles with wooden slatted seats. On return, the loco went on to Treorchy to work the Ocean Sidings for Parc and Dare Collieries. It was on this turn on 18 April 1946 that No.365 was derailed at the Blaengwynfi end of Cymmer Viaduct. The unfortunate outcome was that the engine and leading coach fell over the embankment, No.365 rolling over three times. It was dragged up and went to works for repair. It had not long been released 'good as new' when it ran into a landslip at Trehafod whilst working a Pontypridd-Treherbert 'extra'. An unlucky loco indeed!

Given the gradients in the locality, it was inevitable that from time to time runaways occurred. One of the more spectacular was on 14 June 1961 when sixty coal wagons ran away from Fernhill at the top of the valley. The wagons ran as far as Treherbert; there they were diverted into an empty siding by an astute signalman but all landed in a large heap. The amazing thing with this incident was the number of 'near misses' that happily ensured nobody was actually hurt. The lampman was out of his lamp room and up a signal post, the Carriage & Wagon staff were working on a Saturday 'Ninian Park' set but had left it before it was struck and the Engineers bridge gang had gone for their lunch!

Pwllyrhebog Incline

Treherbert shed was responsible for the incline and the locos that worked it. Of the three Taff Vale 0-6-0Ts (Nos.193, 194 and 195) two were employed on the incline while the other shunted at Tonypandy Yard. 'Normal' pannier No.7722 was the spare engine with the haulage attachment and covered the Tonypandy job if necessary, not

Class 'H' 0-6-0T 794 (195 from February 1949) is in the centre, well cleaned and awaiting its next tour of duty at Pwllyrhebog. To the left, note the back of the 56XX in original condition, before the recess has been made in the top of the bunker to take the upper lamp iron. This modification commenced in 1934/35.

normally venturing onto the incline. Harry House worked at Treherbert shed for many years and remembered a coach load of visitors from Birmingham one Sunday who collected ten shillings for him as appreciation for shunting one of the incline locos out of the shed for them to photograph. This, Harry says, was more than he earned for the day's work! Most work on the incline was done on the early turn and a job remembered well is the twice weekly greasing of the haulage rope by Treherbert staff.

Domestic Arrangements
The turntable was an essential part of the shed facilities despite the allocation consisting entirely of tank engines. As across all the valley lines, engines went chimney first 'uphill' which meant turning the engine if it came off a Cardiff job and went on a Swansea one.

Locomotive coal came from Ferndale which burned with very little ash and made no clinker. The danger was that it could burn the firebars and a sprinkling of sand was necessary to prevent this. Great Western Colliery at Tymawr also provided briquettes for fuel. No.2 shaft winding engine there was built by Swindon Works when the railway

owned the colliery. Railway coal was unscreened, it saved the pennies, and two return trips to Barry would empty a 56XX bunker!

Strange Workings over the Years
In pre-grouping days there was a Cardiff Queen Street-Aberystwyth service via Treherbert, the Afan Valley, Swansea District Line and the Manchester & Milford Railway, 10.05 from Cardiff and 3.23pm from Aberystwyth. During the Great Depression of 1929-1933 (though its effects in the coalfields were much more protracted) many families moved from the Rhondda to the Slough area to find work and of course returned from time to time to see their friends and relations.

On 24 December 1937, there was a 3.10pm Paddington to Treherbert via Newport, Caerphilly and Pontypridd returning at 3.25pm on the 27th December by the same route. Locos were changed at Newport. As late as 1948/49, similar trains were still running. If tender locos came through that were too long for Treherbert turntable, they were returned to Pontypridd to turn on the triangle.

On 17 December 1965, a collision on the South Wales main line at Bridgend resulted in a Circus train

being diverted from Briton Ferry via Treherbert, possibly a first and last.

Rundown of the R & SB and Tunnel Closure
From 13 June 1960, to avoid costly repairs to Gelli Tunnel and Croes Erw viaduct, trains between Cymmer and Blaengwynfi were diverted over the GWR line. That summer, the two stations at Cymmer Afan were replaced by one new island platform. Passenger services from Bridgend to Abergwynfi were diverted to Blaengwynfi.

On 3 December 1962 the line closed to passengers between Briton Ferry and Cymmer Afan, bringing an end to Swansea-Treherbert services. These were replaced by extending the Bridgend-Blaengwynfi services through to Treherbert.

On 26 February 1968, Rhondda tunnel was closed 'temporarily' as a safety precaution and buses instituted in lieu of trains for that portion of line. The tunnel lies below 1,000 feet of rock with coal seams above and below the bore. Subsidence had distorted the tunnel profile necessitating the installation of steel rail ribs and timber lagging over a distance of about 900 feet from the east end and at two places totalling 500 feet half a mile from

The Machine Shop at Treherbert just two months old, fitted out with all that was needed to keep a fleet of tank engines 'on the road'. Clean, tidy and light – indeed, so new that the kettle in the right-hand corner has some way to go to acquire that ancient, black, encrusted look.

the same end. It was, however, a very serious distortion one and a quarter miles from the east end that finally brought about permanent closure, on 24 August 1970. A replacement bus lasted until 'formal procedures' were completed on 14 December 1970.

Up to Date

Since 1981, the Pontypridd-Treherbert line has been single north of Porth and 'Valley Lines'

The south end of the shed on 3 July 1949 with three Taff Vale 0-6-2Ts and the ever-present 56XX. The middle locos are 'A' Class 303 and 365, both locals. 303 looks to be 'next off' as the engineman is oiling round; an unreadable duty disc is attached. The tall water column is one for the modellers.

provides a basic half hourly passenger service to Barry Island. Inevitably there are changes at 'peak' times with some services terminating at Cardiff Central and at Penarth. There is also an early morning service to Aberdare, reversing at Pontypridd. Five trains stable overnight at Treherbert. The Ferndale line lost its passenger service in June 1964. There is no longer any freight traffic on the Rhonnda lines, the last being an engineer's train to recover rails from the Maerdy line on 6 February 1994.

Thanks to the Welsh Railways Research Circle Archives and to Colin Chapman in particular for all things Taff Vale. The standard History 'The Rhondda Valleys' by E.D. Lewis was invaluable.

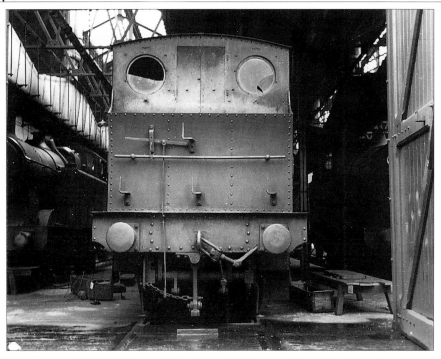

Taff Vale 'H' class 0-6-0T 195, one of the Pwllyrhebog Incline engines, stored in Treherbert shed on 8 August 1951. It had been made 'redundant' a month earlier with the closure of the Incline. It gives a good view of the haulage rope attachment. Photograph W. Potter.

A Treherbert passenger working at an interesting location. Passenger turn 'B', as indicated by the disc above the buffer, covered (among other trains) the 6.16am Treherbert-Penarth and 8.42am Penarth to Merthyr at this time and perhaps it is the latter train that we see. The location is Pentyrch Crossing, in 1949 and the locomotive is recorded as 5617. It was a Cathays loco and in this case would be covering the job. Just to complicate matters further, and to emphasise the amount of 'cross coverage' involved, Abercynon men relieved this job at Pontypridd and worked the Treherbert turn to Merthyr. As to Pentyrch Crossing, the tramway connecting Pentyrch Iron Works and Melingriffith Tinplate Works was here first, arriving by 1815, at least a quarter century before the 'Taff'. Originally narrow gauge, the tramway was 'standardised' about 1871. The works line was in use until about 1959 and was removed a couple of years later. Pentyrch Crossing box behind the loco dates from 1901. The single track in the flat crossing is in need of a little care and attention.

This is what Treherbert was all about. 5687, a resident from July 1958 until November 1962 is just back from Caerphilly Works. This was one of the green '56s' for some years. The date is Sunday 19 June 1960 and a BR standard 'non-corridor' set stands alongside ready for 2Z10 to perhaps Barry Island or Porthcawl. Photograph Alec Swain, The Transport Treasury.

Above. Ferndale was a sub-shed of Treherbert and dated from 1884. The collection of 'cabins' and huts between the shed and the river are worth a second look. The shed itself was 'rationalised' in the early 1930s with two bays of the original four demolished. One open track was retained (on which the 56XX is standing) but an office block covered most of the other. At the same time, this corrugated-clad coaling shelter was provided. It looked a bit out of place at such a small shed but was much appreciated given the weather in the Valleys. There was a turntable at the north end of the shed until 1938 – Ferndale indeed boasted a couple of Dean Goods 0-6-0s in earlier years. The wagons on the left are on the site of the Middle Fan Pit and the lines that once led up to the Cambrian Wagon Works. The signal to the right of the 56XX is a nice specimen with a route indicator.

Right. Treherbert had two sub-sheds (or 'outstations' in earlier parlance); Ferndale and a little one road shed at Pwllyrhebog. This actually stood at Incline Top, Blaenclydach. Of 1919 vintage, it was clad in corrugated iron and housed locos working the Incline. The building behind is officially 'Incline Top Ground Frame', the control cabin for the ropes. The left-hand line is the headshunt, and first part of the zigzag route for trains reversing and proceeding towards Blaenclydach Goods and Clydach Vale Colliery. The cubicle to the right of the telegraph pole amount to 'the facilities' for the shed. The Mile Post on the left reads 19 miles from Cardiff Bute Road, Taff Vale style.

Yet More Tests

When B1 4-6-0 61353 was completed at Darlington Works in September 1949 it differed from all its sisters in that it was specially adapted for testing a variety of exhaust arrangements. To allow for these tests the chimney and adjacent anti-vacuum valve were mounted on a detachable plate, forming part of the top of the smoke box, thus allowing different chimney and exhaust cowl arrangements to be fitted relatively easily. It was envisaged that four different arrangements would be tried, along with of course, the standard configuration which the B1s had when built. The alternatives were the Kylchap, Lemâitre, LMS type double blast pipe and a double chimney with diverging blast nozzles. As events turned out, it was not until October 1950 that any tests were organised, and the engine was 'allocated' that month to the Rugby Testing Station (four week period ending 7 October 1950). As well as static tests on the plant there, controlled road tests were undertaken between Carlisle and Skipton, during the spring and summer of 1951. The locomotive had been at Keith shed and finally

arrived at Rugby from Darlington, where doubtless some attention had been given to it, on 29 December 1950.

There is no evidence that any of the four *'experimental'* exhaust arrangements listed above were ever fitted to 61353, seen in these two views on the rollers at Rugby on 12 June 1951 – road tests took place in April and August, and the engine appears to have been on the rollers both before April and between April and August. Several alterations were made to chimney cowl and blastpipe dimensions but it was found that the standard arrangement was *'about right'*, if the engine was fired to its *'liking'* – i.e. with a relatively thin fire. Apparently the engine kept normal passenger timings over Settle-Carlisle with 436 tons. This was not bad at all for a Class 5, as I believe these were Class 6 timings.

The alterations to chimney cowl and blastpipe dimensions seem to have been undertaken both before and after the static tests. In view of the high hammer blow from the reciprocating parts, the engine was temporarily re-balanced, such that 70% were balanced for the duration of the static tests. This was to

prevent excessive loads being transmitted to the test plant itself, but so far as I have been able to ascertain, such modifications do not seem to have been undertaken on any other engines tested at Rugby; it would be interesting to learn more about this. The locomotive is said to be doing the equivalent of 70 mph in the photographs; notice the instrumentation and the fact that the die block is almost in the centre of the link, indicating a cut off of around 15%. I doubt readers will be able to discern the removable section in the smoke box, as this is only just about noticeable on the original photographs.

The results of the tests were certainly inconclusive, and as far as I can tell no alterations were either recommended, or undertaken on this engine or any others of the class. On completion of the tests in August 1951, the engine was transferred from the Scottish Region to the North Eastern Region (four weeks ending 11 August 1951) and allocated to Darlington. It was finally withdrawn from service in August 1965.

Notes by Allan C. Baker

You'll Remember those Black and White Days...

BLACKFRIARS: WRIT LARGE IN STONE

The great prize for the main line railway companies south of the river Thames was to be able to serve the City of London in their own right with their own terminal station rather than working services over the lines of other companies. The London and South Western muffed it and the London, Brighton and South Coast only managed to gaze at the delectable City from across the river. The South Eastern got to Cannon Street after the lesser London, Chatham and Dover had established, in December 1864, a temporary station at Little Earl Street near Ludgate Hill and in so doing brought the first railway service to the City from south of the river. In due course came Ludgate Hill proper then Holborn Viaduct and in May 1886 St Paul's.

The river crossing had been extended to seven tracks and on the north bank a terminal station, St Paul's, facing on to Queen Victoria Street was constructed. This had three terminal lines in addition to the through lines to Ludgate Hill and Farringdon. The terminus of St Paul's reflected the depth of the LC&D's pocket – or perhaps its lack of depth. It was a two-storey building, with dormers in the roof, of five bays with a turret (tower is too grand a description) at each end. To add some embellishment to this plain façade the lower level was decked out with stone pilasters (above and at street level was in brick) around the two entrances and three windows with the names of various towns or cities, for which one could presumably purchase a ticket and commence one's journey, incised in the stonework. There were, in total, 54 names ranging from Antwerp to Wiesbaden set out as in the accompanying table. The disposition of these lists were:

Column 1	East side of east doorway
Column 2	West side of east doorway
Column 3 and 4	Between the three windows
Column 5	East side of west doorway
Column 6	West side of west doorway

Of these columns, nos.3 and 4 related to home stations, the others being foreign destinations. In general names followed in alphabetical order. Exceptions were Milan/Lyons in column 1, Dresden/Darmstadt and Vienna/St Petersburg in columns 2 and 5 and Sittingbourne/Sheerness and Westgate-on-Sea/Walmer in column 4. For some unexplained reason Herne Bay acquired a hyphen in its name.

D.W. Winkworth

Part of the façade at the west end of the east door and the easternmost of the windows. This 1966 view reflects the unkempt state of the building.

St Paul's was renamed Blackfriars in February 1937 when the London Underground station called Post Office took the name of St Paul's. Redevelopment of the station took place in the 1970s when it was decided to retain the stones with their evocative names. They were gathered together in one large panel in the precise order that they had originally been set. This panel was erected inside the station rather than externally and a plaque commemorating the opening of the new building was unveiled by the then Lord Mayor on 30 November 1977.

	ANTWERP	ASHFORD	GRAVESEND	DARMSTADT	
BALE	BADEN-BADEN	BECKENHAM	HERNE-BAY	FLORENCE	NICE
	BERLIN	BICKLEY	MAIDSTONE	FRANKFORT	
GENOA	BOULOGNE	BROADSTAIRS	MARGATE	GENEVA	PARIS
	BREMEN	BROMLEY	RAMSGATE	LAUSANNE	
MILAN	BRINDISI	CANTERBURY	ROCHESTER	LEIPSIC	ROME
	BRUSSELS	CHATHAM	SEVENOAKS	LUCERNE	
LYONS	CALAIS	CRYSTAL PALACE	SITTINGBOURNE	MARSEILLES	TURIN
	CANNES	DEAL	SHEERNESS	VIENNA	
NAPLES	COLOGNE	DOVER	WESTGATE-ON-SEA	ST PETERSBURG	VENICE
	DRESDEN	FAVERSHAM	WALMER	WIESBADEN	

You'll Remember those Black and White Days...

Above. A 1971 view showing the incised stones around the doorway (still with elderly Southern Electric sign) in Queen Victoria Street. At the right is part of the bridge carrying the railway to Holborn Viaduct.

Left. The relocated stones formed into a panel in the new station building. November 1977.

ENIGMA

KEITH MILES first visited Bletchley in the war years. Only in Britain would The Great Secret on which hung, maybe, the very fate of the Nation, hide behind a fence, some trees and an engine shed...

My initial encounter with Bletchley was as a young lad during the war years. It took the form of an exploratory excursion with a fellow Kings Langley fence-topper (see *North of Watford* BRILL January 2001) in order to give substance to a name. For Bletchley was only a name to us – the northern destination of most of our locals and, therefore, a place of some importance perhaps? Yet my pre-war gazetteer recorded a population of only 866 as compared with Kings Langley's 3,335. Furthermore, the atlas indicated connecting lines extending both east and west yet the name did not carry a 'Junction' suffix as did our Watford and Willesden.

It was a minor puzzle, maybe even an enigma...

On the day, as our train slowed for the run in, our attention was drawn to the brickworks on the down side with its array of kilns surmounted by tall chimneys. Then immediately after that there was a triangular junction with a flooded clay pit at its centre. The northern leg of the triangle was, of course, the double track Oxford/Banbury branch but it transpired (D.S. Barrie's *Euston and Crewe Companion,* Oakwood Press 1947) that the southern single track leg was first laid when, in 1854, the LNWR inaugurated a through express service to Worcester and

Wolverhampton via Yarnton and the 'Old Worse and Worse'. (The Oxford, Worcester & Wolverhampton Railway). The service was withdrawn in 1861 in favour of the Great Western route and the formation lay derelict until 1934 when part of it was used for a connection into the new Fletton's brickworks. By the time of our visit the whole curve had been re-established for wartime traffic, troops and materials, and, as it happens, was retained after the end of hostilities for goods traffic with the coincident development of Swanbourne Sidings.

However, back to our train which rattled over points and crossings before drawing to a stand in the station. Quickly surveying the scene to discover the best vantage point, we found an eight-platform station with the main buildings on the down side and a goods shed and yard on the up side. Beyond the lines of the Cambridge branch there were

Left. Camden's 46247 CITY OF LIVERPOOL hurries through what seems to be a deserted station apart from a couple of spotters on platform 4 one of whom is making an entry in his book... shades of our visit some fifteen or twenty years earlier! Then, of course, the engine had been clad in a streamlined casing painted sombre plain black, a livery that it had carried from the outset, being built in 1943. The casing was removed in May 1947. Photograph Bryan Wilson, The Transport Treasury.

extensive freight sidings. Also on the down side, south of the station, was a carriage shed and, just north of the station buildings, an engine shed and yard bounded at the rear by a bank and a belt of trees. Although we didn't know it at the time, these shielded the grounds of Bletchley Park where boffins from 'the Ministry' were struggling with another Enigma, the German cipher machine.

But how had this busy place developed in the midst of almost open countryside? Well, the railway came to Bletchley in 1838 but, not unnaturally, the minimal first station was only classed as 'intermediate' and appeared in the London & Birmingham Railway timetable of 1840 as 'Bletchley (& Fenny Stratford)'. This acknowledged the much larger settlement to the east athwart Watling Street, pre-war population 4,602. The station was enlarged in 1846 on the opening of the LNWR, as it had then become, branch to Bedford. Further enlargement took place with the inauguration of the Buckinghamshire Railway's lines to Banbury in 1850 and to Oxford in 1851. The portico on the station front dated from this period. In 1862 the Bedford services were extended to Cambridge but meantime traffic on the main line had increased to such an extent that a third up goods relief line was brought into use between Bletchley and Primrose

Hill, in 1859. Quadrupling was inevitable, however, and the construction of new tunnels, particularly those at Watford, 1874 and Primrose Hill, 1878, permitted four lines right through to Euston by 1879. In the same year, incidentally, the Buckinghamshire Railway was absorbed by the LNWR which had, in fact, worked it from the outset.

Nonetheless, a contemporary plan of Bletchley showed the four lines reducing to three through the station. This situation was not to remain for long, however, because a major rebuilding scheme took place in 1881 in conjunction with the completion of the Northampton loop and the provision of four tracks between Bletchley and Roade. The scheme resulted in the platform layout that we had found on our visit and which was to remain for a number of years. The original subway connecting the platforms was abandoned in favour of an overbridge and an extensive range of buildings was constructed on the station front.

The most impressive of these was a small hotel built in the grand Tudor style with stone mullioned windows set in diaper* patterned brickwork beneath Dutch gables. Then, around the Buckinghamshire

---

*ornamental design of diamond reticulation ('arranged with intersecting lines') for walls, etc

The station approach in February 1950 with the sometime hotel on the right now labelled as 'fully licensed dining and tea rooms'. Just beyond this building a British Railways Ford 10 van is parked outside the Parcels Office whilst, nearer the camera, a Wolesley Series 3 seems to have travelled abroad. The smoke chutes of the engine shed can be seen above the Post Office building across the end of the station yard.

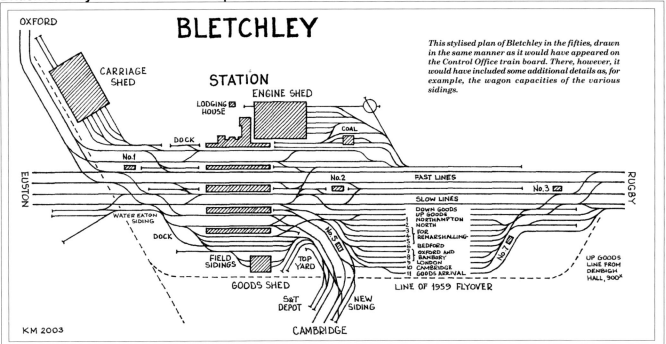

BLETCHLEY

OXFORD

CARRIAGE SHED

STATION

ENGINE SHED

LODGING HOUSE

DOCK

No.1

EUSTON

WATER EATON SIDING

DOCK

COAL

No.2

FAST LINES

No.3

SLOW LINES

DOWN GOODS
UP GOODS
1 NORTHAMPTON
2 NORTH
3 FOR
4 REMARSHALLING
5
6 BEDFORD
7 OXFORD AND
8 BANBURY
9 LONDON
10 CAMBRIDGE
11 GOODS ARRIVAL

RUGBY

UP GOODS LINE FROM DENBIGH HALL, 900x

FIELD SIDINGS

TOP YARD

No.5

No.7

LINE OF 1959 FLYOVER

GOODS SHED

S&T DEPOT

NEW SIDING

CAMBRIDGE

KM 2003

This stylised plan of Bletchley in the fifties, drawn in the same manner as it would have appeared on the Control Office train board. There, however, it would have included some additional details as, for example, the wagon capacities of the various sidings.

Railway portico, came various station offices of similar design to the hotel; though in plain brickwork they had decorative finials on the gables. Beyond them rose a simpler, unaffected two storey building housing, in part, a Post Office. Within the next few years other buildings appeared across the end of the station yard which were taken over by the Royal Mail for post and sorting offices. The building which they had vacated was then occupied by the United Kingdom Railway Temperance Union and the Railway Servants Coffee Tavern Company which, between them, provided a recreation room and library on the first floor and a committee room and coffee tavern on the ground floor. The latter, known universally as the 'Coffee Knob' was to continue dispensing welcome beverages for nigh on eighty years.

The first engine shed was a timber affair built for the coming of the Buckinghamshire lines but it collapsed during a gale in 1872. It had three roads with the tracks passing through and converging into a single track dead end adjacent to the office and lodging house. Of distinctive construction, it stood across the station yard from the Booking Office. Two storeys high, it was topped by a large water tank for loco supplies, the water being pumped from a purpose built reservoir in the angle of the main

A closer view of the station yard with two Royal Mail vans, a Morris Z and a larger Morris Commercial, parked outside the Post Office. Alongside the Coffee Knob, still proclaiming itself to be a 'Temperance Refreshment Room', are a pre-war Austin 7 and its Austin 8 successor produced during the war.

You'll Remember those Black and White Days...

An impression of the old lodging house with its roof-top tank. Originally housing the shed offices, it became an eight bed 'barracks' for enginemen on lodging turns but was latterly used to accommodate Polish shed staff. The term 'barracks' was, in this case, particularly appropriate since they were all ex-soldiers. We had a band of them on each ashpit shift at Willesden – some had been quite high ranking officers.

line and Oxford branch (our supposed flooded clay pit) which attracted the inexplicable sobriquet 'Newfoundout'. (A.E. Griggs, *A Railwayman's Tale of Old Bletchley,* Baron Burch, 1996). Incidentally the lineside apparatus for the down TPO

was installed atop the bank of this stretch of water, reached by an angled path up from Water Eaton Road then along the cess – quite daunting, I should imagine, for a postman on a dark and windy night for the passing of the 'Down Special'. But to continue...

The six-road shed that we found dated from around the same period as the station reconstruction but was not the Webb 'New Standard Steam Shed' northlight roof pattern. Rather it followed the style of the 1866 shed at Coventry in that it had an arched entrance to each road beneath two gabled roofs. It was to be re-roofed in 1954 with a so-called 'lightweight' structure of steel rails, troughing and patent glazing. The arched doorways disappeared at the same time. The facilities included a typical Nor'West coal stage beneath a large water tank, also supplied from 'Newfoundout' but a supplementary source had since been found in wells at Fenny Stratford. In the mid-1930s a water softening plant was added and, much later, two further storage tanks were erected beyond the turntable, each mounted on a dozen tall columns, the tank over the lodging house having by then gone out of use.

The shed had been coded 3 in the LNWR list but in the LMS scheme

of 1935 it became 2B, a garage shed of the Rugby District. At the end of the war it boasted an allocation of sixty-nine engines of which over 70% were still of LNWR origin. There were no less than twenty-eight 'Super Ds', albeit most of them of the 6F class G1 variety, nine 'Prince of Wales' 4-6-0s, four 'Cauliflowers', four 'Coal Tanks' and three 1P 2-4-2Ts. To these were added one 'Black Five', ten Stanier 2-6-4Ts and four 'Jinties' plus a Midland 2F and, believe it or not, four Lanky A class 0-6-0s which acquired the local nickname of 'Gracie Fields'. An opulent collection one might think but, in addition to main line commitments there were six branch lines to service with some of the locos outstationed at sub-sheds at Oxford, Leighton Buzzard, Newport Pagnell and Aylesbury.

Its importance was recognised in 1946 when the Rugby District was sub-divided and Bletchley was given the status of a main depot with Northampton as its garage shed. This became evident to me when, at the Crewe Divisional Office in early 1950, I had to include Bill Bellamy at Bletchley in the morning telephone conference of District Superintendents. Later that year it acquired the new individual code of 4A (Shrewsbury having been transferred to the Western Region)

The Buckinghamshire Railway portico contrasts with the surrounding LNWR buildings, built of a similar, but plainer, style to that of the hotel. The symmetry of the design is blighted, however, by the unfortunate staircase tower to the footbridge – I'm sure that HRH would call it a carbuncle. The grubby Hillman 10 van on the left is put to shame by the gleaming 1947 Hillman Minx salon being gazed at so wistfully by the lady passenger. Did she arrive by bicycle and will she and the riders of the various other bikes in the picture make use of the mounting block at the foot of the left hand column?

The entrance to the Booking Hall, which must have been so familiar to the cryptanalysts and many other personnel at Bletchley Park – Station X. Not only did Bletchley have direct links to London but trains went east and west to the two ancient universities where many of the 'boffins' were recruited – see the wonderful evocation of Bletchley (its *drabness* for instance) and distant trains in Robert Harris's marvellous wartime novel *Enigma*. It was just as well that, in my experience at least, most trains of that era were trouble free and ran to time – all part of the war effort!

by which time the allocation had changed radically. There were still twenty-four 'Super Ds' (but 7F class G2 or G2A), two 'Coal Tanks', a 2-4-2T plus the original four 'Jinties' but the remainder comprised four 4F 0-6-0s, six 4MT 2-6-0s, six 'Black Fives' seven 8Fs, two 2MT 2-6-2Ts and a mixed bag of nine 2-6-4Ts. They were also saddled with the 'branch line design' diesel 10800. All good things come to an end, however, and March 1952 saw the shed taken into the Willesden District and recoded 1E.

It's nearly half past one on Thursday 27 April 1950 and through the other door of the Booking Hall can be seen the tail end of the 1.34 to Oxford standing at platform 2. To the right of the doorway appears a list of all timetabled train departures commencing 12 September 1949 whilst through the archway to the left, leading to the stairs to the footbridge, is a summary of certain up trains and a list of fares. In the first ten months of 1952 140,000 passengers had been booked and 1,800 season tickets sold. In addition, forwarded parcels totalled 27,100 consignments and received parcels 24,500.

Through the door into the station itself and onto platform 1. The large number of various velocipedes would seem to indicate the absence of a cycle shed for either passengers or staff. The ends of the three island platforms had the normal LNWR canopies but the central portions had a more copious covering; almost a train shed but, in fact, only the footbridge was fully protected. Behind the gas lamp in the foreground is an example of the minimal station signing inherited from the LMS.

I had come to know the area more intimately in the early summer of 1949 when 'firing on locomotives in service' as an Improver at Willesden. At that time there were over fifty daily freight trains leaving the London area for the north. There were fifteen class C or D fitteds, mostly in the evening but including the famed 2.55pm ex-Camden 'Doodlebug', but the remainder were largely class F or H. The fitteds ran through Bletchley with the crews on lodging turns; for the rest, however, it was a different story. Former Rowsley locoman George Newton reminiscing about that era said, 'O'course in them days there were

In 1954 the engine shed behind platform 1 was rebuilt from its original twin gabled roof design with arched doorways for each of the six tracks into the simpler form shown here and a stone tablet on the fascia, unseen in the haze, commemorated the event. The date is May 1965, the final year of its life – the last steam engine belled of the shed on 5 July. Nonetheless, when it was all swept away there was left behind a remnant of the past in the shape of the retaining wall on the right built from L&BR stone sleepers. A vast concrete stop block which once stood guard at the 'run-off' opposite the main approach road to the turntable is also still there, broken-backed and doubtless an object of mild curiosity to those drivers who care to give it a second glance. The mouldering steps which once led up to the water tank are also visible in the undergrowth. Photograph Colin Stacey, Initial Photographics.

DOWN MAIN LINE PASSENGER TRAINS COMMENCING 10th. SEPT. 1951. UP

DOWN

arr.	dep.	
1·15	11/54	x Euston, all stations
	6·22	Northampton, all stations
7·28	6·24	x Watford, all stations
7·46	7·50 6·40	Euston-Windermere & Workington
8·7		Rugby, all stations
9·17 9·33	7·30	Euston-Northampton, all stations
10·55	9·10	x Euston, all stations
11·52 11·56	10·50	Euston-Crewe, limited stop
1/1 1/4	12/0	Euston-Birmingham, limited stop
1/20		Rugby, all stations
1/52 1/54	12/20	Euston-Northampton, all stations
3/2	1/35	x Euston, all stations
4/10 4/14	3/5	Euston-Northampton, limited stop
4/42	3/47	x Watford, all stations
5/42	4/15	x Euston, all stations
6/33 6/35	5/27	Euston-Rugby, limited stop
6/40 6/43	5/6	Euston-Northampton, all stations
6/51	5/26	x Euston, all stations
7/8	5/43	x Euston, all stations
7/24 7/27	6/6	Euston-Northampton] selected
7/34	6/12	x Euston } stations
8/5	6/42	x Euston, all stations
8/21 8/22	7/15	Euston-Perth, sleeper
8/41 8/44	7/15	Euston-Northampton, all stations
11/25	9/55	x Euston, all stations

UP

arr.	dep.	
3·44 3·55	5/40	Glasgow-Euston, sleeper
4·44 4·54	12·10	Liverpool-Euston
6·48		Euston, all stations
6·55	(Set down only)	Stranraer-Euston, Boat express
7·8 7·13	7·0	Wolverton-Euston, all stations
7·30		Euston, limited stop
7·39		Euston, all stations
7·43 7·55	6·55	Northampton-Euston, all stations
8·15		Euston, all stations except Watford
8·38 8·40	8·0	Northampton-Euston, limited stop
9·4 9·8	6·40	Wolverhampton-Euston
10·32 10·35	10·0	Northampton-Euston, non-stop
10·56	9·50	x Rugby from Bletchley
10·45		Euston, all stations
11·21 11·26	8·20	Liverpool-Euston
12/40		Euston, all stations
2/24 2/34	9·10	Llandudno-Euston
3/15 3/20	8·20	Carlisle-Euston
4/53 4/59	3/40	Rugby-Euston, limited stop
5/10		Euston, all stations
6/27 6/30	5/7	Rugby-Euston, all stations
7/59	6/57	x Rugby, all stations
9/37 9/41	7/40	Birmingham-Euston, limited stop

BRANCH LINE PASSENGER TRAINS COMMENCING 10th. SEPT. 1951

OXFORD-CAMBRIDGE

	Bletchley arr.	dep.	
		6·40	Cambridge
6·25 x Oxford	7·31		
		7·54	Bedford
7·15 x Banbury	8·22		
8·0 x Oxford	8·58		
		10·19	Cambridge
		11·10	Bedford
10·15 x Oxford	11·17		
		12/15	Cambridge
		2/5	Bedford
1/40 x Banbury	2/46		
		3/40	Bedford
2/42 x Oxford	3/46	3/55	Cambridge, Limited stop
		4/25	Cambridge, Limited stop to Bedford
3/42 x Banbury	4/51		
		5/5	Bedford
		6/15	Woburn Sands
5/20 x Oxford	6/24	6/36	Bedford
		7/15	Bedford
6/55 x Oxford	8/2		
6/55 x Banbury	8/9		
		8/28	Cambridge
		9/0	Bedford
10/30 x Oxford	11/33		

CAMBRIDGE-OXFORD

	Bletchley arr.	dep.	
		5·24	Oxford limited stop
6·15 x Bedford	6·59		
7·27 x Woburn Sands	7·40		
		8·0	Banbury
7·52 x Bedford	8·26		
7·37 x Cambridge	9·16		
		9·30	Oxford
10·00 x Bedford	10·38		
9·30 x Cambridge	11·10		
		12/15	Oxford
11·18 x Cambridge	12/53		Limited stop from Bedford
12/45 x Bedford	1/27		
		1/34	Oxford
		2/22	Banbury
2/5 x Cambridge	3/42		
4/0 x Bedford	4/46		
		5/5	Oxford
		5/28	Banbury
5/15 x Bedford	5/58		
4/40 x Cambridge	6/16		Limited stop from Bedford
6/33 x Woburn Sands	6/44		
6/13 x Bedford	6/58		
6/15 x Cambridge	7/55		
		8/15	Oxford
		10/0	Oxford, limited stop

relief cabins everywhere – cabins wi' a gang of men in waiting for trains'. And so it was; despite the slow freights being destined for distant parts, Overseal, Hugglescote, Beeston, Humberstone Road, Desford Junction and so on, few of the crews got past Bletchley, the trains stopping at No.3's home signal for 'exchange of trainmen'. The Willesden sets then went across to the relief cabin off the end of platform 8 and contacted control to find out which of the trains coming up the slow line or piling in on the goods line from Denbigh Hall they should relieve for the return trip south.

The LNWR had set up a local control office on platform 8 in 1913 covering the area Tring to Rugby (exclusive) but the immediate post-World War II years saw the completion of the overall LMS scheme and the work passed to the London (Western) District Control Office housed in the 66 Drummond Street building at Euston where I spent a couple of months on placement in the early summer of 1950. The area covered was the main line and branches up to Ashton signal box (exclusive) between Castlethorpe and Roade. So far as Bletchley was concerned the Yard Inspectors had to report the loading of freight trains and advise the Control Room at the beginning of each shift the 'detailed position of traffic on hand including goods brake vans, empty stock and crippled wagons waiting acceptance by the shops' (*Operating Control Organisation, LMS 1947*). Bletchley No.2, the biggest of the signal boxes with 108 levers, had to report the 'arrival, departure or passing of freight trains, selected and special passenger trains and light engines, including arrival of engines off freight work and special empty coal trains at and departure of all engines from the Motive Power Depot'. No.3 box, half its size, had the responsibility of reporting 'departures of freight trains and light engines from the Up and Down Goods Lines'.

For the Motive Power Department, the shed's Running Foremen had to advise Control of 'the number and home depot of the engine, the signing on times and home stations of the enginemen for all classes of trains including scheduled re-manning, except passenger and in certain instances coaching stock trains; also the names and times on duty of men brought on for relief purposes or conducting'. A similar task was carried out in respect of goods guards by the Yardmaster's Office and these procedures recognised that, whilst passenger services largely ran to time, freight services of that era did not. One of Control's functions, therefore, was to ensure the minimum of staff overtime and, in particular, that men were able to catch their next turn of duty; there had to be a minimum of twelve hours between booking off and signing on again. The return working off 'The Doodlebug', for example, Willesden turn 806 after lodging at Crewe, was the 5.5am class E or 'Maltese Cross', due at the High Level Sidings at 11.55. On the two occasions that I worked it I booked off at 2.50pm the first time and 4.30 the second time having been relieved at Nuneaton and finishing the trip 'on the cushions'. It was with some wry amusement that, whilst in the Control Office, I saw the same service being pegged up on the train board at Bletchley almost spot on time each morning – it was being worked by one of the diesel twins, 10000 and 10001, and was obviously being given the road!

I have tabled the weekday main line passenger services for the period commencing 10 September 1951 from which it will be seen that, despite its branch connections, few express trains called at Bletchley. Intending passengers had to travel by the stopping trains from Euston or, if coming from the north, change at Rugby and proceed forward by one of the locals. I understand that more expresses called in pre-war days and, indeed, there was a fatal collision on Friday evening 13 October 1939 involving two of them. The 7.37pm Euston to Inverness sleeper was standing in the down

The rather gloomy staircase ascending from the Booking Hall to the footbridge. At the head of the stairs is another reminder of the times, a poster on behalf of the Lord Mayor's National Thanksgiving Fund offering people a 'chance to say 'thank you' for food gifts from overseas'. Although it's nearly five years after the war, rationing is still in force on some commodities. I was living in Crewe during this period and can remember a small shop in Gresty Road where two jars of not very appetising sweets were labelled as being 'off points' ... a chance to eke out the sugar ration.

fast platform and in the process of having a van attached to the rear by 9169, when it was ran into the following double-headed 7.50pm Euston-Stranraer boat express, also due to stop. This was actually in the first weeks of the war when blackout was in force, there was no moon and heavy rain was being driven across the tracks by an east wind. The eleven coach Stranraer, headed by 5025 and 6130 THE WEST YORKSHIRE REGIMENT had passed Tring six minutes late but arrived at Bletchley three minutes before time. It was evident, therefore, that despite the wartime imposition of an

overall maximum of 60mph, an average of about 70mph had been maintained after passing Tring to the site of the collision. None of the crew members of either engine, for whatever reason, saw any signals after the colour light distant for Stoke Hammond, some three miles out and which was clear, although a partial brake application had been made on the approach to Bletchley. The first indication of impending doom was the explosion of detonators at the No.1 inner home at which the train should have stopped until the platform was available. An emergency full brake

application was made but too late; the train, at an overall weight of over 600 tons and travelling at an estimated 25 to 30mph, smashed into the Inverness, 5025 and 9169 meeting smokebox to smokebox. The Super D destroyed its van and the two rear coaches of the sleeper (fortunately they were brakes) mounted the wreckage and crashed over onto the down fast platform, demolishing the waiting and Refreshment Rooms. 5025 followed it and a large portion of the station roof was brought down. Providentially, a member of the platform staff had glimpsed the lights of the approaching express and the sparks flying from the full brake application and was able to shout a warning to those working in or around the stationary Inverness and most were able to leap clear. Nevertheless there were four fatalities, including the driver of 9169, six seriously injured and around three dozen with minor injuries. (Accident Report, Ministry of Transport, December 1939).

Most stopping trains used platforms 5 and 6, 3 and 4 being on the fast lines. I worked several of the locals with both Willesden and Watford engines and men, mainly on 2-6-4Ts but the 4.15pm ex-Euston was booked to a 5XP, either a 'Jubilee' or a 'Patriot', because the return working, after putting the carriages away and turning and watering on the shed, was a parcels train back to Euston. Although it left Bletchley with only a handful of bogie vans, by the time it had attached at several places en route there were up to eighteen hanging on the tender at Willesden. The other odd thing about the 4.15 was its variable make up; on three successive days it had seven, eight and six bogies.

Platforms 1 and 2 were allocated to the Oxford/Banbury trains and were known locally as the 'Oxford Bays' although both of them were, in fact, through platforms with the lines shown in the Sectional Appendix as 'Permissive Block' between Nos.1 and 2 signalboxes. In practice the trains were generally brought into platform 2 leaving the other track clear for shunting movements and light engines to and from the carriage and engine sheds. In addition the locals to Rugby invariably left from the north end of platform 2.

Platforms 7 and 8 were used by the Cambridge trains and all the points and signals at the north end were worked from No.5 signalbox which also controlled the south end of the eleven-track marshalling yard. The other end of the yard had No.7 and the nearby No.3 was another main line box. No.4 was further

Descended now onto platform 4 and looking across the fast lines to platform 3. In the centre of the large notice board at the foot of the stairs is a blacked out (or very grubby) LMS 'Hawkseye' pattern station sign. Beyond the waiting rooms can be seen the inevitable Wymans bookstall, the cast iron gents toilet and, dimly beneath the canopy, the coal stage in the loco shed yard (see also *True North Western Style*).

round the Cambridge branch towards Fenny Stratford; there was no No.6. An atmospheric picture of this area around the time of our visit has been drawn by former locoman A.E. Grigg in his *Country Railwaymen (Blandford Press, 1985)*. It finishes off a chapter concerning a night train to Cambridge in somewhat inclement weather. 'On reaching Bletchley the train backed into the shunting yard after the remaining mail bags had been loaded on No.8 platform. In the darkness the loud voice of the shunter could be heard shouting instructions to the signalman in No.5 box. 'Four, six and on the shed' bellowed the dark figure holding a pole and a hand lamp; it is doubtful if anybody other than the signalman would have understood. By a combination of sounds, hand signals and knowledge, the signalman in his dimly lit box knew what was required. The swing of the shunter's lamp, a white then a red, the changing of signal levers and some wagons rolled into No.4 road and some into No.6. Then off came the semaphore signal and the engine was away across the main lines on to the loco shed and a wet, irritating night was nearly over.'

As will have been gathered from my *True North Western Style,* BRILL January 2003 and *They used to set on fire!,* BRILL March 2003, the branch line trains were in the hands of the LNW 'Prince of Wales' and 'Cauliflowers' at that period but peace time brought the 'Flying Pig' 2-6-0s and they and the 2-6-4Ts took over the services, to be superseded in due course by DMUs. By the by, the LMS 3-car articulated diesel train was introduced into public service on the branch lines in the autumn of 1938, albeit experimentally, but failed on several occasions and was moved elsewhere at the end of the year – see *Diesel Dawn, The Limousine,* BRILL January 2002. Oxford Rewley Road station was closed in October 1951 and the trains diverted into the former GWR station. The Banbury branch was cut back to Buckingham in January 1961 but even those services were withdrawn in September 1964 followed by those to Oxford in January 1968. At the same time services were withdrawn between Bedford St Johns and Cambridge and the trains were eventually diverted into Bedford Midland.

In 1952 the station had a post-war renovation scheme visited upon

it including electric lighting in place of gas, redecoration throughout in regional colours and improved ticket and parcels offices within the original buildings. One new structure, however, was a 'modern style' brick-built refreshment room and stationmaster's office on platform 4/5. Apart from these the scene remained much as it had been before but the 1955 Modernisation Plan saw the construction of what some people saw as a white elephant, the Bletchley flyover. This was built to carry traffic both from the north and from the Cambridge lines, across the main lines into the Oxford branch in connection with the proposed extensive redevelopment of Swanbourne Sidings into a major marshalling yard. The latter was put a stop to by Gerry Fiennes, newly appointed Chief Operating Officer at the BRB, who was firmly convinced that such yards should be located in the principal areas of production and consumption rather than in green fields. So, as he commented in *I tried to Run a Railway'* (Ian Allan 1967) 'The Bletchley flyover remains as a memorial to the people who failed to see that railways must live by concentration, not dispersal.' These

Bletchley's 42062 arrives at platform 5 with the terminating 5.10pm SO from Euston on 26 September 1953, framed by an array of signals. The post-war renovation scheme of the previous year has resulted in enhanced electric lighting and an improvement in the station signs. 42062 was one of a couple of Fairburn tanks that arrived from Stoke at the end of 1951 in exchange for a pair of Fowlers. In the summer of the following year most of the remnants of the original allocation were replaced by five BR Standards, new from Brighton. A further five came in the summer of 1954 and these ten monopolised the services until the end of 1959. Then came a widely-resented move to concentrate the Fairburns on their 'home' Region, swapping SR examples for LM BR 4MT tanks, usually in better nick. The Bletchley BR engines were displaced by half-a-dozen Fairburns from the Brighton District but even these gradually dwindled away, the last to go being 42105 and 42106, to Willesden in December 1964. Photograph B.K.B. Green, Initial Photographics.

days, as it happens, the flyover is the only means of reaching the former Oxford lines, the ground level tracks having long gone.

It was the electrification of the West Coast Main Line that finally saw the greatest changes, in 1965. A comprehensive reconstruction scheme had the carriage and engine sheds and all the station and platform buildings, including the footbridge, swept away. Even platform 1 disappeared to have new station buildings erected on the site with a walkway access to platform 2 whence a new footbridge sprouted. The engine shed site inevitably became a car park but a reminder of an historic past is still there for all to see; the retaining wall at the foot of the Bletchley Park Bank is made up of London & Birmingham Railway stone sleepers.

I was around when all this was taking place (1965, not 1838) since I was involved in the construction of the new Power Signal Box, commissioned in June the same year and taking over from Watford PSB at Cheddington and handing over to Rugby at Hanslope. During this time I came across Dick Mansell who'd been appointed as Station Master. I'd previously known him as a Traffic Inspector at Rowsley and we'd shared the same digs for several months. And here's another

Crossing now to platform 6 and looking across the slow line tracks at the Refreshment Room on platform 5. Beneath the gas lamp it can be seen that one of the notice boards has been used to display the new British Railways totem. The signs on the left hand door, labelled 'Refreshments' are confusing because the middle one says 'Closed' and the bottom one says 'Open'! It would appear that trains are expected on both the up and down fast lines.

enigma; every night, without fail, when he opened the door to the stairs, he'd say 'I'm off up the wooden hill to Bedfordshire'. Actually, that's not a bad idea ... goodnight!

The inside of the Refreshment Room, the counter dominated by a large Stotts water boiler for producing the elixir of life. I used this and other similar establishments quoting the magic formula 'OCS', that is 'On Company Service', which entitled me to a penny off the price of a cup of tea. At this period, 1951, when the price was only thre'pence (just over 1p in new money) the discount was significant but as it rose to sixpence and more (horror!) it was less so. Today's cuppa is more like £1 but my annual salary as a Running Foreman in those days was only £432.

You'll Remember those Black and White Days...

Moving back down island platform 6/7 with a view of both the slow and Cambridge branch lines. I suspect that those are staff motorcycles and I also suspect that the porter on platform 5 is stubbing out his cigarette in the sand-filled fire bucket.

Finally a glance across the Cambridge branch tracks to platform 8, adorned like platform 1 with a collection of bicycles. Notice that, also like platform 1, it has no canopy beyond the 'overall' roof. In the distance parcels vans can be seen against the loading dock although parcels are beginning to accumulate on platform 7.

While the crew take their ease on the platform, 47500 simmers at the head of a parcels train in platform 7 – probably the one that was the return working of the Willesden engine and men off the 4.15pm ex-Euston. Note that 47500 is equipped with carriage warming hoses and headboard brackets above the buffer beam of the type formerly used on LT&S and North London trains. In fact, this engine came to Bletchley from Devons Road in March 1954 and the Jinties from that shed regularly worked the Broad Street-High Barnet services in pre-war days before steam was ousted by London Transport Northern Line trains. Photograph P. Gomm, The Transport Treasury.

Willesden 8F 48658 draws a class J freight out of the marshalling yard across to the up slow line in February 1953. Despite the mineral or empty wagon headcode it seems to be a mixed train. Beyond the engine is the big No.2 main line signalbox whilst on the right is the smaller No.5 box. Incidentally, Bletchley's four Jinties were occupied in shunting at the north and south ends of the yard (both 24 hours), the goods shed and nearby sidings (daylight only) and the carriage shed and station, around sixteen hours. To the far left in the picture is the curiously high but shallow pair of water tanks, demolished in the early-1980s, fronted by the shed's 15 ton steam breakdown crane, No.1025. Photograph K. Barrow, Initial Photographics.

It's December 1959 and the bulk of the flyover is beginning to take shape between the carriage shed and the Oxford branch. Viewed from the incomplete deck of the flyover, Wellingborough's shop-soiled 92085 creeps past a 15mph restriction sign with a great hole in the tender coal and leaks from a variety of glands. When the L&BR arrived at Bletchley there was nothing to the east of the tracks except open countryside but housing development began in the late 1870s with Duncombe Street, seen beyond the train, and over the decades Bletchley and Fenny Stratford grew together. Both have now been swallowed up by the creeping cephalopod that is Milton Keynes. Photograph R.C. Riley, The Transport Treasury.

You'll Remember those Black and White Days...

Bottom left. From the other side of the incomplete flyover, a view north towards the station, interrupted only by the exhausts from a number of locomotives including 48668 running light past No.1 box. Beyond the roof of the carriage shed is the Station Master's house and the flat roofed building in front of it is the Staff Association Social Club which came in very useful during the construction of the Power Signal Box in the open ground opposite. About the same time underbridge No.153, Buckingham Road/Queensway, just beyond the closeboard fence, was rebuilt to afford a wider carriageway. Photograph R.C. Riley, The Transport Treasury.

Left. An unidentified 8F brings a freight across the now completed flyover. Buckingham Road/Queensway on its new widened alignment goes under the first arch whereas the original path was under the second. The sometime cattle clock appears to have been rebuilt but is only home to a Triumph Renown of 1948/9 vintage. Photograph P. Gomm, The Transport Treasury.

Below. Production diesel traction on the West Coast Main Line was initiated in May 1959 by the arrival at Willesden of a trio of new EE Type 4s, D210-D212. The two seen here hauling the 6.40am ex-Wolverhampton on August Bank Holiday Monday 1961 are D302 (train engine) and D318, built November 1960 and February 1961 and originally allocated to Crewe North but transferred to Camden in May 1961. The steam age is still in being, however, as witnessed by the column of smoke from an engine in the carriage shed yard and the two LNWR water columns on the ends of the platforms. Photograph Michael Mensing.

Twice A Test Bed!

Motor coach M28220M at Morecambe Promenade in 1955. M28221M is in the background. These ex-LNW units were fitted with an air braking system, rather than the vacuum brake of the original MR sets.

This fascinating series of photographs illustrate a long-abandoned part of the national network which was electrified on the overhead line principle TWICE, once by the Midland Railway and much later by British Railways. This was the Lancaster, Morecambe & Heysham line which the Midland Railway first electrified in 1908 on the 6.6kV a.c. system. The Midland thus became the first user of a.c. traction current in this country. It was planned as a test bed for a proposed main line scheme from Derby to Manchester, a purpose it was to serve again much later as we shall see. Seven new vehicles were built at Derby, three 60ft 72 seat motor cars numbered 28610-28612 and four 43ft control trailer cars 29290-29293 seating 56, all with an open saloon layout.

The Midland trains rumbled on until 1951 when they were judged to be life-expired and replaced by push-pull steam trains. The motor coaches and two remaining control

trailers were taken to Horwich Works were they were dismantled. As only two of the four control trailers made that last journey, this may explain the adaptation of coach 22202, seen in the photographs.

However, British Railways were considering the electrification of the West Coast Main Line (WCML) in

the early 1950s and the line was destined to become a test bed or proving ground yet again, still at 6.6kV but at 50 cycles rather than the 25 cycles of the Midland Railway system. Most of the MR overhead structures were basically sound but one stretch of the line at the Lancaster end was selected to test

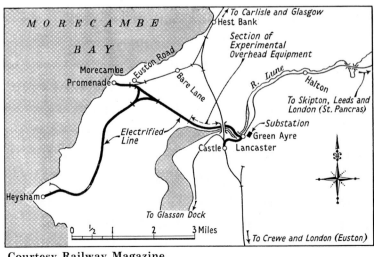

Courtesy Railway Magazine.

You'll Remember those Black and White Days...

Lancaster Green Ayre in 1947 and a three car train, with a Midland motor car leading. The pantograph identifies it, possibly, as 28610 which had Westinghouse equipment. The others, 28611-28612, had Siemens equipment and bow collectors when new, although photographic evidence suggests that they later received replacement pantographs. Certainly 28611 had one in 1948. Alongside the pantograph on the roof a board can be seen, which reads 'It is dangerous to touch this apparatus'. A forerunner, if understating the matter somewhat, of the 1960s warning flashes. The overhead gantry supporting the catenary has an isolating/earthing switch at the left-hand end which appears to be open, with manual controls at platform level. Something very similar can be seen on the 25kV network today.

a variety of structures made by British Insulated Callenders Cable (BICC), which later were to be a feature of the WCML proper. The 'new' rolling stock was to be of LNWR origin since, fortuitously, the four trains which had become redundant when the 630v dc third/four rail Willesden Junction-Earls Court service ceased in 1940 had been in store ever since, probably at the Mitre Bridge Depot at Willesden Junction. Although similar to the stock used on the Euston/Broad Street-Watford services they could not be used in multiple with the Oerlikon units nor the later 1927 compartment sets, hence their long period of storage, perhaps with a view to a resumption of the service after the War.

Motor coach M28222, the last of the conversions (1956) showing that the original panelling and ventilation louvres immediately behind the driving compartment were retained. This was no doubt due to the provision of underfloor electrical equipment on this vehicle; the original equipment compartment thus did not need modification, another example of the 'minimum-cost' nature of the project. The speedo drive can also be seen, on the rear axle of the bogie.

Thus BR had a 'minimum-cost conversion' and three of these ex-LNWR trains were re-equipped at Wolverton Works with English Electric (EE) transformers, rectifiers and traction motors with either a pantograph or Faively collector and took the place of the steam service in August 1953. The fourth set was re-equipped with underslung Metropolitan-Vickers equipment, as an alternative to the EE equipment which was housed within the motor coach and entered service in 1956. These four trains maintained the service until January 1966 when the whole system closed and the route was abandoned having served its purpose. Lancaster Castle station had to wait until March 1974 before it saw another electric train, this time on the WCML. The LNW sets were numbered:

One of the sets leaving Heysham, carrying the earlier BR 'Lion & Wheel' emblem. Note the original MR overhead gantry.

Driving Trailers	29021-29024	56 seats
Trailers	29721-29724	62 seats
Motor Brakes	28219-28222	28 seats

* 28222 seated 38, made possible by the underslung equipment.

M28220M in 1955 waiting to leave Heysham. Observe the wonderful 'blanking covers' for the marker lights. There are double outwards-opening doors to the luggage compartment (shown open here); the hand-operated sliding door just this side of it was marked 'Guard' – the first two letters, 'GU' are just visible.

Trailer car M29021M at Lancaster Castle in July 1955. Without the lowered roof of course, the sets presented a wholly different, and much more antique look. Even with the refurbishment inside, the advancing years of these sets could not be hidden.

Train arriving at Morecambe platform 3 with passengers waiting to board. Peculiarly, what looks to be a Royal train coach (six wheel bogie) is standing on the left. The manual sliding doors were passenger-operated and one wonders what modern safety regulations would make of these – though they also featured on the Oerlikon stock and on the London Underground. The pile of ashes reveal a liberal attitude to fire cleaning in the station precincts.

Right. Set leaving Heysham in 1955 (frustratingly the numbers were not on the ends at first). Later, speedo drives appeared on the leading bogies of the Motor Brakes, attached to the rear axle.

Below. Lancaster Green Ayre in 1955. The view is along the electrified single track (note the novel wooden ducting) between Green Ayre and Lancaster Castle station. The substantial and curving metal bridge over the Lune is the electrified 'main line' to Morecambe and Heysham. Green Ayre shed lies hidden behind those wagons – note the Crab with smokebox door open, on the coaling/disposal roads.

Bottom right. The original Midland 'OHL' (as the authorities came to term the overhead line) was solid no-nonsense turn of the century stuff. These original posts, incredibly, are wood telegraph poles, with a clamped steel supporting cross piece between. It was termed 'wood pole and steel bridge portal construction'. It seems crude to us but had the great virtue of utility and low cost at the time – and who's to say it looks any less elegant than efforts of decades later?

Left. The questions BR were pursuing in 1953 would hardly be answered by old telegraph poles. A variety of new materials were becoming available and the configurations of OHL equipment tried out from 1953 involved all sorts. A length of some 4,000 feet of the original Midland OHL (see plan) on the 'main line' was taken down and replaced by a variety of 'light, hinged cantilever structures, separate for up and down lines'. This was designed to carry 20,000 volts for, rightly, it was thought that a.c. electrification would generally be carried out at a much higher voltage than the 6.6kV originally installed, which had been retained for convenience. This view illustrates just two types – concrete and steel frame – that were tried out. There were several other configurations. The 4,000 foot 'test bed in the test bed' was carefully chosen so that it experienced the harshest of conditions; there were curves and straight stretches, the coast brought variable weather conditions and steam traffic would subject the wires to blast and corrosion. It was the intention that comparative tests should be made on the different materials as well as the various protective treatments applied.

Below left. Green Ayre station in July 1955. The cylinder under the buffer beam is a reservoir for the braking system.

Below. Wonderful cab view, showing the heavy duty windscreen wiper (BR had still to get these right when main line diesels arrived half a decade later) and the driver's adjustable/removable mirror – which he presumably took to the other end with him! Observe also the air-operated warning 'whistle', just to the right of the wiper.

FOURUM
On the Kingsbridge Branch

Pannier tank 3796 arrives at Brent, the junction for Kingsbridge, with the branch train on 17 July 1956. The branch platform was on the south side of the main line; this curves away to the left while the branch disappears to the right. Photograph R.C. Riley, The Transport Treasury.

Gara Bridge, the only crossing place on the line, in the summer of 1961. The train about to cross 5525 and its single coach was another single carriage, a diesel car; these had been introduced the previous April but steam was still needed on additional summer Saturday trains. Photograph Peter Barnfield.

A 2-6-2T, 5525, pulls away from Kingsbridge station with a six coach through train for Paddington in the summer of 1961. The idyllic Devon countryside was of course one of the many attractions for holidaymakers and it is not surprising that the branch had its quota of camping coaches. Photograph Peter Barnfield. For a thorough, excellently illustrated account of the line and its glories see our sister organ RAILWAY BYLINES March 2003. £3.50 post free (while stocks last) if you quote this article!

For a West Country lad like Peter Kerslake, opportunities to see LMR locomotives were few and far between. Fortunately a holiday with relatives in Lancashire allowed two day trips to Crewe from Manchester. Readers may recall some of the bounty of that time in the pictures of DUKE OF GLOUCESTER and Coronation Pacifics in the September 2001 issue of BRITISH RAILWAYS ILLUSTRATED – here are a few more. Captions by Allan C. Baker

Right. The up 2.10pm from Liverpool (the sometime 'Manxman') heavily loaded and approaching Crewe on 1 June 1956. The train connected with the Isle of Man Steam Packet Company 9.0am departure from Douglas, due Liverpool 1.0pm and ran non-stop to Euston, due at 5.45pm. The locomotive is a grimy Edge Hill Princess Royal Pacific, 46211 QUEEN MAUD; it had been at Edge Hill since 1943, but over the next few years moved several times to Crewe North and back again. The time here is 2.55; observe a tender full of coal for the journey south, and a wisp of steam from the safety valves as the train heads along the No.4 Down Through Road. The tall building in the murk is the Grease Works where, among other things, oil and grease was recovered from cotton waste and rags, gathered from all over the LMR. Photograph Peter Kerslake.

Below. A trio of 'Fresh Off Works' ('FOW' in Crewe parlance) engines, passing along No.1 Through Road at the north end of the station on the afternoon of 31 May 1956, on their way to the South shed. From left: Jubilee 45641 SANDWICH, Patriot 45537 PRIVATE E SYKES VC and 2-6-4T 42599. This was a regular sight in the early afternoon at Crewe, eagerly awaited by us 'spotters' as we might get sight of a locomotive from a distant part of the LM, or indeed another Region altogether. The Jubilee was from Nottingham and therefore in the first category; the Patriot was from Carlisle Upperby and the tank from Longsight so both would be familiar sights. Things rebounded similarly on Peter Kerslake – the engine for the return to Manchester on the second day, though 'FOW' was so-familiar Laira Britannia, 70016 ARIEL! It was standard practice for 'FOW' engines to go to the South shed first – there is little or no coal in the tenders, for the Works would only put enough in for testing purposes. Photograph Peter Kerslake.

Below right. On the afternoon following the 'FOW' trio the Patriot is back, standing on No.2 Through Road, waiting to take over a train from the south. This would be the engine's first job after overhaul and would take it northwards towards its home shed. Crewe South would work freight engines away in the direction of 'home'; passenger or mixed traffic types went to the North shed for a period of running in. There was a 'Works fitter' in permanent residence to attend any minor adjustments; he would also visit the South shed as necessary. In my time the fitter was a fellow called Frank, but while I can see him now I cannot recall his surname! Photograph Peter Kerslake.

You'll Remember those Black and White Days...

Two Days at Crewe
Photographs by Peter Kerslake

Left. Princess Royal Pacific 46208 PRINCESS HELENA VICTORIA, backing off Crewe North ready to take over the 8.0am ex-Plymouth-Liverpool train, 1 June 1956. Due in Crewe at 3.49pm and away again at 4.0, the train was doubtless a filling in turn for the Edge Hill Pacific, normally used exclusively on that shed's London workings. She is just about as grimy as her sister, 46211. A pleasing vista of the station entrance, with a Patriot on a train in No.1 Platform. Photograph Peter Kerslake.

Bottom left. Upperby's 46126 ROYAL ARMY SERVICE CORPS with an afternoon parcels and empty stock train, about to leave Crewe from No.2 Through Road on 1 June 1956. The amount of coal in the tender suggests it had come on the train here, and would be working back to its home shed. Notice the 'special' reporting number W708, and the missing sandbox filler cover just to the rear of the nameplate – some nice wet sand in that box! Photograph Peter Kerslake.

Below. The familiar view from the famous footbridge over the lines at the north end of the station, a haven for all 'spotters'! Princess Royal Pacific 46212 DUCHESS OF KENT, a Crewe North engine and about a grimy as its Edge Hill sisters, is about to set off north with the fifteen coach Birmingham to Glasgow train on 1 June 1956. It was due away at 1.0pm, having left Birmingham at 11.25; the Pacific would have come on the train here with extra coaches doubtless added – note the full tender of coal. We already have right of way, the illuminated 'F' on the route indicator adjacent to the signal showing a routing from No.1 platform on to the Down Fast. North from Crewe to Winsford Junction there were four tracks. Photograph Peter Kerslake.

You'll Remember those Black and White Days...

A special working arriving at Crewe from the North Wales line on the morning of 1 June 1956, behind rebuilt Patriot 45545 PLANET of Camden. The train has some of the Royal Train vehicles; 'word on the bridge' was that the Duke of Edinburgh and his entourage were travelling back to London from a visit to a Scout Camp in Snowdonia. Unlike the Edge Hill and Crewe North Pacifics, PLANET is (understandably) clean. The train appears to be working under the 'Deepdene', rather than 'Grove' arrangements, hence the normal express headlamps. 'Grove' normally meant either the reigning Monarch or Heir to the Throne was on board, and carried the four head lamp code; 'Deepdene' arrangements were for lesser mortals, and engines carried the ordinary express head lamp code. Photograph Peter Kerslake.

The No.2 Through Road and a non-stop up Elder Dempster Line Ocean Express Boat Train on 31 May 1956, behind Camden's 46146 THE RIFLE BRIGADE. This special working (note the W497) would have run in connection with the sailing of one of the line's ships from Liverpool. It would not be advertised to the general public but only to boat passengers through the shipping line's own publicity. Quite a few such trains operated on both the LM and other Regions, connecting with sailings. The driver has clearly put on steam again after coasting through Crewe, with the fireman doubtless adding a round to the fire. The building to the left on No.3 platform is the famous 'Coffee Tavern', open 24 hours a day and, while ostensibly for staff, was frequented by all 'in the know'; I've spent many a happy hour in there! Photograph Peter Kerslake.

Birmingham Interlude

On 2 May 1959, 6008 KING JAMES II waits to leave Snow Hill with the 2.10pm Paddington-Birkenhead. The BR 4MT 4-6-0 on the right, 75026, had piloted the train from Leamington Spa, due to a 5mph speed restriction in force at that time immediately south of Snow Hill tunnel. A lot of piloting had been necessary at that time (for a week or two) until the work was done; the restriction meant a severe check at the foot of the incline, so that single engines could not get the necessary 'run-up'. Photograph Michael Mensing.

Something of a contrast over at New Street. On 18 February 1961 a Black Five stands in the back sidings (Platform 11 in foreground) with a train of vans. A wonderfully atmospheric view. Photograph Michael Mensing.

Descent to Carmont

A4 Pacific 60034 LORD FARINGDON in its Scottish exile, in the last year or so of its long life; it carries the Ferryhill 61B shedplate indicating the period to be post-May 1964, when this Southern Area stalwart had transferred to the Aberdeen shed. It had only gone to Scotland for the first time, to St Margarets, in the autumn of 1963; before that it had spent most of its first twenty-five years at Kings Cross or Grantham. It might be late but the A4 looks in perfect nick, passing the photographer to plunge down the dip to Carmont. While in England, 60034 had a corridor tender but in 1963 it got FLYING SCOTSMAN's after the A3's withdrawal for preservation – so that's 60103's streamlined non-corridor tender in the picture. 60034 has also been recently repainted at the lower front (60009 had similar treatment at the same time) and has lost her works plate. The 'tree' sign is a warning of 'forest ahead' and not to make sparks. Photographs The Transport Treasury. Thanks to Tony Wright in preparing these notes.

You'll Remember those Black and White Days...

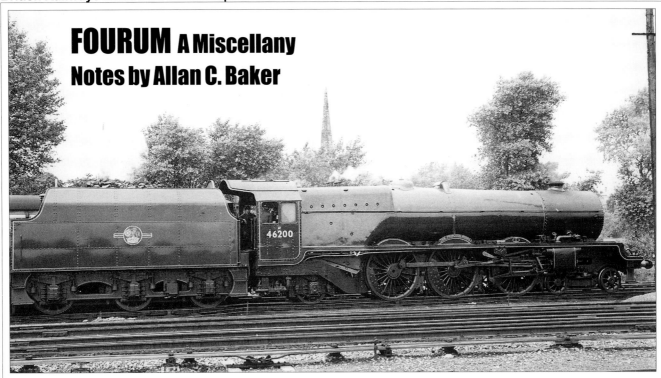

FOURUM A Miscellany
Notes by Allan C. Baker

The original LMS Pacific, 46200 THE PRINCESS ROYAL, in BR maroon livery with the LMS style lining. It is probably at Shrewsbury, in the sidings adjacent to the shed and would be waiting to take empty stock into the station for a return working. In store for two winters, it was allocated to Crewe North for the summers of 1960 and 1961 and Carlisle for its last season in 1962. Its condition suggests it is working an enthusiast special of some sort, in 1961 or 1962 perhaps – can any readers help? It is in forward gear, and doubtless about to move off. Although the turntable at Shrewsbury was not big enough, these engines could use the triangle at Severn Bridge, east of the station. Photograph The Transport Treasury.

Ivatt 2MT 2-6-2T 41241, waiting to leave No.6B bay at Crewe with a stopping train for Wellington, in July 1963. The Crewe-Wellington trains were always worked by Wellington engines and men, though in earlier times some had been sub-shedded at Crewe for the workings. The Ivatts had displaced ex-GWR pannier tanks on the jobs some years earlier, but the summer of 1963 was to be the last, passenger services terminating from 9 September. The engine is in reverse gear; this would suggest that it has just arrived from Gresty Lane shed, where engines working both passenger and freight services over the route to Wellington via Market Drayton were still serviced. This former GW outpost also closed when the passenger service was withdrawn, and some of the displaced men were transferred to Crewe North. Photograph D.H. Beecroft, The Transport Treasury.

The first BR Standard 4MT 4-6-0, 75000 at Swindon Works, presumably awaiting some sort of attention. It was allocated to Swindon shed and along with the rest of the class of eighty, had been built there too. It migrated to Shrewsbury in September and remained there until going to Tyseley in August 1959. Photograph D.H. Beecroft, The Transport Treasury.

Lastly, a mystery location. The engines are Britannia Pacific 70006 ROBERT BURNS, with a Carlisle Kingmoor shedplate (it had gone there from Stratford in December 1963 and remained until withdrawal in July 1967) and BR Standard 84028. The 2MT had come to the LMR, initially to Newton Heath, in September 1961 from the Southern Region at Eastleigh. The 2-6-2T went to Skipton in October 1961 and was effectively withdrawn from there in December 1965. I say 'effectively' for, with several others of the class, it was nominally transferred to the SR in November 1965. They were, ostensibly, bound for the Isle of Wight but this transfer never happened and the idea of them replacing the ageing O2s on the island came to nothing. I cannot help thinking that this picture must have been taken at Carlisle, but don't recognise the surroundings, unless it is the extreme south end of the yard at Kingmoor, and the wall to the right is supporting the entrance road, which did connect with a roadway that crossed the lines at a higher level. The tank would not normally work as far north as Carlisle; perhaps it had come for attention of some sort. Note the young spotter looking over the wall! Although the smaller Standard engines had conventional dome mounted regulators as opposed to the smokebox mounted ones on the Pacifics, to keep the footplate layouts consistent with a 'pull-out' arrangement of control, the regulator rod was external to the boiler, as can be clearly seen in this view. Note too, the speedometer; the drive can be seen from the trailing crankpin. Photograph The Transport Treasury.

DIESEL DAWN
Finishing Touches

There was a time when diesels were rolling out of our various works as if there was no tomorrow, if that's not mixing metaphors. Observe this beautifully new, pristine 204HP shunter, literally 'rolling out' with another – though doubtless posed – ready behind. It's frustrating that there's no date to the photographs and doubly so that the number of the little loco cannot be seen. A retrospective case for 'smokebox' numbers perhaps? The first of these built at Doncaster (known at the time, peculiarly, as the DJ15 class) was D2044 for the North Eastern Region; this was turned out on 29 November 1958 with D2045 and D2046 following on 6 and 13 December. D2047-D2051 were all under construction before the end of the year and by the end of 1960 Doncaster had completed nearly seventy, up to D2113. This last one appeared on 23 December 1960, completing the Doncaster batch. In the close-up picture the fitter is adjusting the sight glass which shows the water level in the radiator – you can see it in the other pictures, high up on the engine's right-hand side.

'Baby Scot' No. 5987, later 5504 ROYAL SIGNALS, in the paint shop at Crewe Works, probably after completion in 1932. It was renumbered 5504 in 1932 and named ROYAL SIGNALS in 1937.

A Hundred Miles By Bike to Mecca – the Story of Basil Spencer
Introduction by Edward Talbot

In his article on the LMS CORONATION nameplates (BRILL Volume 9 April 2000) Michael Brooks described Basil Spencer as the 'doyen of nameplate collectors'. Not being a nameplate collector myself, I did not know Basil until one day, soon after the publication of my book *LNWR Miscellany* in 1978, I received a letter from him. Quite possibly it arrived in a recycled envelope, as described by Michael, but inside was some nicely printed notepaper with a photograph at the top of an LNWR 'Prince of Wales' going well on the 2pm 'Corridor'. After congratulating me on the book, he said, 'I loved everything about the LNWR. I saw all the 'Georges', all the 'Princes' and all the beautiful 'Claughtons'. I still think that the 'Claughtons' were the most handsome of all locos.'

After that we corresponded occasionally and I also discovered that Basil had a reputation for fair dealing in his nameplate activities. As I found his letters so interesting, I eventually suggested that he should write up his reminiscences. It was no great surprise to discover that he had already done so in 1980, as a result of a similar suggestion from an old friend, and shortly before his death on 19 March 1989 he sent me a copy. Here then is the railway autobiography of Basil Spencer, doyen of the nameplate-collecting fraternity, great enthusiast and gentleman.

A History of H. B. S.
Describing some of the exploits, antics and adventures of his early (glorious) days.
It all started at two o'clock in the morning on Tuesday 19 September in the year 1911, when I came into this dreary world at 92 Jockey Road, Sutton Coldfield. I maintain that WILD DUCK emerged at the same time. Six Georges were built in the September and WILD DUCK was the fourth, so there is little doubt that we emerged together.

In the spring of 1915 my father bought a house – DUNKELD, 1 Royal Road, Sutton Coldfield, about three miles from Jockey Road. Even today, I can well remember peeping through the bedroom curtains with my mother, one winter's day early in that year, and watching German prisoners of war marching past; they were camped nearby in Sutton Park.

Although I was then barely four years old, I remember there was something really wonderful about our new house. At the bottom of our garden there was a railway; not only that, but it was on a very high embankment, surely the best of all views. Furthermore, we were almost at the summit of a very hard and steep climb.

Over the next twenty-one years I was to see some of the most exciting and spectacular trains of my life. For the first eight years we were there, this line was purely Midland but after the Grouping in 1923 we used to get many LNWR and even L&Y engines, and I grew up loving the Midland and the LNWR as much as

You'll Remember those Black and White Days...

any railways in the land. I adored the Midland engines. To a boy there was something very beautiful about red engines, and the LNWR 'blackberry' black too was so much more beautiful than any black used by other railways.

At the time of the Grouping, the LMS had an enormous variety of locos but there was not much variety on the GWR. There were a few other things I did not like about GWR engines too. They had taper boilers, which I never liked(!), and they had no domes. To me they always looked unfinished. The Midland and the LNWR engines had beautiful domes.

A thing I always disliked about so many GWR locos was those dreadful long iron bars, which seemed to be for holding the buffer beams up! They must have been quite six or eight feet long and quite two inches round, and were fitted to almost every class other than express locos and very small tanks. I do not think any other company ever fitted anything so ugly. Nevertheless, of course, I loved them all!

My father used to take me to watch GWR trains near Hatton, and we used to see many Stars, Saints and County 4-4-0s, which I loved, but I never really liked their tank engines or goods engines. The exceptions were the County Tanks, which I thought were very beautiful. When I was about six I travelled on a train from Snow Hill to

Bournemouth behind LA FRANCE; I remember that well. However, so much for 'God's Wonderful Railway'.

I must have spent 95 per cent of my younger days observing the LMS and 5 per cent observing the GWR. I spent YEARS on New Street and just now and then I would walk over to Snow Hill. When I was on Snow Hill, I would worry a great deal about what I might be missing at New Street; but when I was on New Street, I never worried about what I might be missing on Snow Hill!

The line at the bottom of my garden was the Midland Railway from Birmingham to Walsall. All the carriages, and all the passenger engines, were in the beautiful Midland red, and absolute cleanliness was the order of the day. The local passenger trains were hauled by the very pretty little 0-4-4 tank engines or by my old favourites, the big 0-6-4 tanks. We used to set our clocks by the trains, yes, even by the goods trains.

We used to get a lot of 'specials' including 'City of Birmingham Gas Dept' trains, fully laden, running from Birmingham to Liverpool and Manchester. Though always double-headed, most of them came to a stop right outside our house. There was always a great deal of shouting and bad language among the four men and they would usually stand for about ten minutes, cleaning the fires and stoking up.

We also used to get a lot of Fyffe's banana trains running from Avonmouth Docks, Bristol, which used to use our line in order to avoid Birmingham on their way to the north. I remember one winter's day when a banana train stuck. It was worked by a Midland 7ft 4-4-0 and once it had stopped, there was no moving it. In the end they had to split the train, take the first half up to Sutton Park station and then come back for the rest. We also had a lot of 'Cadbury Excursions' from Manchester and Liverpool. They were usually hauled by the beautiful 'Lanky' moguls, always painted red and always going at full speed. They would return at night, at about eight o'clock, and even if it was dark, mother and I would go outside to watch, and what a sight they were too!

In the summer months of 1925-30 we used to have the 'Pines Express' every Friday and Saturday. Saltley would send two locos up to Walsall and later they would come down with 'The Pines' at top speed, running from Manchester to Bournemouth and cutting out Birmingham

The LNWR also ran through Sutton Coldfield from Birmingham to Lichfield and I often took a walk to watch them. In 1919-20 I used to walk under the LNWR line on my way to school. I usually arrived late, because I used to wait to see a train. It was always hauled by a

'Rebuilt Precursor' 374 EMPRESS at the west end of platform 3 at Birmingham New Street in April 1924, probably on a Liverpool/Manchester train. Photograph H.G.W. Household.

You'll Remember those Black and White Days...

'George the Fifth' 2495 BASSETHOUND near Clifton Road Junction, Rugby, with an excursion train to London.

Precursor Tank and what a handsome engine that was, especially with its train of superb chocolate and cream carriages.

The most wonderful days of all, I suppose, were at that time, after my father bought his motor cycle in 1922. He used to take me to watch the trains at Coton Crossing on the LNWR main line from Euston to Glasgow. It was a very lonely crossing and an extremely fast spot. There used to be a great deal of traffic and most of the trains were going at high speed, especially the up trains. No GWR trains ever fascinated me like those glorious Claughtons did. They have kept a Star. Why didn't they keep a Claughton? There were 130 of them and I saw every one. I also saw every Prince and every George.

The most beautiful of all locos I think were the Midland 4-2-2s and I actually saw fourteen of them. In the 1920s they were usually used as pilots but they were a wonderful thing to see. I always thought they were a nicer-looking engine than the GWR singles, because of the enormous dome, and the great long overlap at the front of the GWR locos.

No Midland compounds ever came into Birmingham before the Grouping, and my friend and I always thought they were the most

beautiful engines in the world. So when the LMS started building them in 1924, and went on to build more in 1925, 1926 and 1927, and even five more in 1932, those were the greatest days of our lives. In 1926 I attended Lawrence's College in Birmingham and I used to go home to Sutton for lunch. I was always five minutes late going back, because I had to watch the 2.30pm London leave. It was usually a brand new compound. All went well for a whole term, but when a new boy arrived, who also came from Sutton and who was always back at 2.25pm, I got into very serious trouble.

That same year I went with the school to London Zoo. We went behind a new Midland compound on a two-hour train which got held up at Coventry. It was a wonderful run, once we got away, and we arrived early. Unfortunately, I did not see the zoo. Somehow I got lost on arrival and found myself at St Pancras. That was my favourite London station. There was a terrible row, but my parents never heard about it.

In 1925, when I was 14 years old, my parents allowed me to cycle as far as Lichfield, nine miles, but 'not a yard further'! However, I am afraid I used to carry on to Derby, some 34 miles. Of course one saw plenty of Midland compounds there. I always

used to go first on to the main road bridge which overlooked the shed and works. There were always several lines full of engines that were either new or fresh from overhaul.

One day in the summer of 1926 the first thing I saw from that bridge was a massive *grey* 2-6-0! It was the only shop grey engine I ever saw in my life outside a works. It had tiny yellow numbers painted on the cab side – 13030. To me it was a most magnificent engine, and I loved all the class till the end of steam. After a while they painted them red, beautifully lined out. The 'Crabs' of course were designed at Horwich and had one or two unique features, such as the regulator handle in a slide. They were about the only LMS engine that Stanier did not spoil, retaining their lovely L&Y chimney till the end. Later I was to see as many as fourteen in one day, at Crewe, all painted red.

One summer's day in 1927 I again looked over that bridge at Derby and there stood the most fantastic loco I had ever seen, 6100. It had just been delivered from Glasgow. I went straight down on to the station, crossed all the lines and climbed up into the cab. I must have spent an hour in that engine – thank goodness I was never seen! It was unnamed at the time but what a

You'll Remember those Black and White Days...

superb thing it was. Later that winter I was to see these Royal Scots running at full speed at Tamworth, one after the other, all day long.

I shall never forget 8 September 1927. It was the day my father came home from the office and said, 'We are going to Blackpool next week for a fortnight. There won't be room for us all in the car, so would you mind going by train?'!!! I was just sixteen years old. Father was an economist, like me, and gave me 6s 6d to get a half-day excursion ticket – not using the return half, of course. I have it all down even now: 345 (LNWR old numbers), an 0-6-2 tank to Birmingham, and 5756 (Prince of Wales) from there onwards. One was not supposed to leave the train until Blackpool but I did some quite dreadful things and got away with them all. I got out at Stafford, did the shed and then got another train to Crewe. I did the North and the South sheds there, and then got a train to Preston and did the shed there too. In no case did I leave the station – I just walked along the lines.

I shall never forget Preston station that Saturday afternoon. There was every type of LMS engine one could wish to see: L&Y 4-6-0s, Claughtons, compounds, scores of those fantastic L&Y 2-4-2 tanks, which used to run very heavy and very fast express trains, the splendid L&Y 4-6-4 tanks and the beautiful Furness Railway 4-6-4

tanks. I arrived at Blackpool very late at night but not too late to do Talbot Road shed. I must say my parents were a bit worried; they were certainly relieved to see me.

Very early on the Sunday morning I walked on to Talbot Road station and there up against the buffer stops, of all things, stood a magnificent L&Y 'Highflyer' Atlantic, newly painted in LMS red too. What glamorous things they were! I saw very little of the sea that fortnight but what a holiday!

In the winter of 1927, my firm closed down and I joined the 'two million'. I desperately wanted a new bike. My father, though a wealthy man, was 'dead tight' and would not give me a penny. I saw an advertisement in the *Birmingham Mail* 'Potato Pickers Wanted'. The address was in Castle Bromwich, so I borrowed a friend's bike and went up there. The old farmer seemed a bit worried and said, 'But you don't look like a potato picker'. I could not think what he meant but he said, 'Right, start here at 8 o'clock tomorrow'.

I arrived at the farm shortly before eight the next morning. There were about thirty men standing around and no other boys like me. They were the roughest and toughest lot I'd ever seen, the lowest of the low, all the dregs of the Birmingham slums. At first I thought they were hobos. We had to climb into the back of an open lorry – it was mid-November and extremely cold – and

were taken to another farm about ten miles away at Lea Marston. Then we were split up into pairs and each pair given a large skip. As the tractor went round and round the field, we had to pick up the spuds and fill the skips. It was terribly hard work. As the tractor never stopped we could not stop either.

Without a doubt it was the most backbreaking work I ever did in all my life. We worked from 8am till 5pm five days a week and we got 25 shillings a week (£1.25). My mother had said that if I could keep it up, I could have the money for my new bike, and believe it or not, my father never knew how I earned that money. Anyway, I kept it up for five weeks and then bought my super brand new Armstrong bicycle. It was the only brand new 'vehicle' I have ever had in my life. Oddly enough I got on well with the 'roughnecks', though our journeys together each day were always done in silence, and we were all too tired to talk during the meal break.

Even in the depth of winter we used to cycle from Sutton to Crewe, 55 miles. It used to take us about four hours and was a very hard ride. Sometimes we would hang on to lorries and once or twice we would do it in under three hours. I remember being on Crewe station just after eight o'clock morning. My word we were keen!

In 1928 when I was 16 I worked at Lucas's in Hockley and I went on a half-day excursion every Sunday

Royal Scot 6100 as yet not named, at Euston in 1927, on display to the public and awaiting naming. Probably only days before, Basil Spencer had been amazed to see this engine new at Derby.

Resplendent in shiny new LMS red paintwork, Compound No.1152 stands at Rugby in September 1925, having just been delivered from the North British Locomotive Company.

throughout the year – London, Manchester, Liverpool, Llandudno, Sheffield, Rugby and so on. I always went shed-bashing alone and the trains never got back until about 2am. I always had to walk home, 7½ miles, getting into bed about four o'clock, and having to be up again for work at seven!

Arriving at Edge Hill shed one Sunday morning in 1928, I was caught by the foreman, who chased me out, literally, shouting that he would call the police. I found another entrance and got in again that way. When I had got to the last row and was about to book the last few, a chap stepped out from between two locos and called out, 'Here he is', and I almost collapsed from shock. To my amazement, he smiled and said, 'How do?'. He had been looking for RALPH BROCKLEBANK and had just seen it when he said, 'Here he is'!

I did Crewe Works for the first time in 1928 when I was 17. I was with a friend and it was late afternoon on a winter's day. The foundry was something never to be forgotten. It was a hive of industry, men were working like slaves and

the noise was fantastic. We went in there to see those amazing little narrow-gauge engines, BILLY, TOPSY, TINY and so forth; they were rushing around like a lot of little bees and we had to take great care, but we saw the lot. They were Ramsbottoms and ran for about seventy years.

The Paint Shop was also a wonderful sight. It was full of Princes all painted red and all with lovely names - GALLIPOLI, ANZAC, MINERVA and PLYNLIMMON were some of them. The Princes were handsome engines and looked magnificent in red. A magical place.

The first five years of Grouping, 1923-28, were fascinating. It took the LMS years to get going. Many LNWR locos were still carrying their LNWR numberplates right up to 1928. That day at Crewe we saw red Jumbos, Precursors, Georges, Princes and Claughtons. Only one Experiment was ever painted red and no Renowns, Alfreds or Jubilees, but there were red 0-6-2, 2-4-2, 4-4-2 and 4-6-2 tanks.

I shall always remember that day. When we left the works, just before 5pm, it was not only dark but very

very foggy. We had been walking all day, round the North and South sheds as well as the enormous works, and we were as hungry as wolves. We had 8d (3.3p) between the two of us and went down a dirty little street and bought a potato pie for 8d. Then we got on our bikes and rode about a mile until we reached the old NSR line. There we climbed down the bank and ate our pie underneath the bridge. We now had rain as well as fog, with 54 miles to go! I remember we got hopelessly lost at a place called Milford, I think it was, and we arrived home just before midnight.

In 1929 I managed to get an AJS motor cycle and one day with a friend on the back went to Derby to do the works. We came out at 5pm to find that the bike had been stolen. So we went up to a policeman on point duty but when I told him what had happened, he told me not to interrupt him; 'Can't you see I'm busy?' and sent us to Derby CID.

The chief of the CID was the greatest bully I have ever seen in my life. All his officers were frightened to death of him. We were shown into his office and he did not

You'll Remember those Black and White Days...

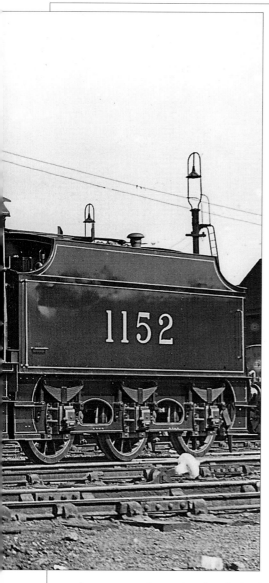

speak or even shout. He bawled at us. It was 6pm, we were 35 miles from home and had not a penny between us. I remember him bawling at me, 'Why didn't you lock the BLOODY thing up?' During our 'interview' an extremely disreputable-looking man was brought in to the room in handcuffs. 'Don't bring that scum in here', yelled the big man. We were there for an hour and a half. Derby CID telephoned the Sutton Coldfield police, who sent a policeman to my house. My mother gave him 10s (50p), the Derby CID gave us 10s, and we caught the next train home.

About a fortnight later the police called at my house to say that my AJS had been found abandoned at Ashbourne, Derbyshire, and I had to collect it. In those days it was not an offence to take away a vehicle – one could say one had borrowed it – but it was possible to prosecute for stealing the petrol. Neither did one have to be insured!

Since then I have had eleven motor cycles and am now driving my 37th car. I was driving a thousand miles a week for a living in the period 1934-39. I have now had 53 yearly

driving licences and must have covered over a million miles. I have a clean licence but have lost count of the endorsements. Wherever I go, I am always in a bit of a hurry, but so far so good!

As early as 1927 I applied for a footplate permit and, of course, was turned down. I made an application at least once a year after that right up to the war but each time without success. In 1947 I started writing for permits again and the LMS this time as good as told me not to write again. In 1959 I was working 'nights', entirely on my own, very close to the Southern main line. My works were situated near Woking and the screaming of those night expresses passing by at 80 or more on their way from Waterloo to Exeter or Bournemouth really set me off! So once again I started applying for a footplate permit. My old friend, the late Colonel Rixon Bucknall, who because of his rank could obtain a permit whenever he wished, had always told me not to ride the footplate for the first time at night. Well, being me, I then felt I must do just that!

This time I had applied to the Western Region and was quite shattered one day to receive my first 'pass'. BR had agreed that I should travel on a Birkenhead-Paddington night express, joining it at Snow Hill at 8pm. The fortnight prior to the run was the longest fortnight of my life...

So it came about that on 28 September 1960 I joined the train at Snow Hill. It was a dark and misty night and I was very thrilled to find we had on a King - KING EDWARD III. Rixon Bucknall had been right. To say it was frightening would be putting it mildly. In fact, had the driver suggested at Leamington that I might ride in one of carriages, I would have done so with very great relief; and had I not taken a whole quarter bottle of neat rum, while waiting in the shadows of Snow Hill station, I should probably not have survived the run! It was an out-of-this-world experience, but once we had cleared Banbury I regained all my confidence.

Having obtained my first permit, I had no trouble at all in getting others. Indeed, I was never refused again. Between September 1960 and July 1963 I had no less than fourteen really glorious runs. My next trip was on the down 'Northumbrian'. I rode on the A3 GALTEE MORE for 106 miles from Kings Cross to Grantham and then on DIAMOND JUBILEE to York. I returned on the up 'Aberdonian' from Doncaster to London on a cold moonlit night.

What superb engines the LNER had! Although the A3s were by far the oldest engines I travelled on,

their riding was the smoothest of the lot, even though GALTEE MORE was clocking 90 just north of Potters Bar. I always thought they were amongst the most beautiful of all locomotives too. After that I had a trip on a Merchant Navy hauling the down 'Atlantic Coast Express' from Waterloo to Salisbury, returning on the corresponding up train.

No one was ever allowed to travel on the footplate without a locomotive inspector to accompany him and so British Railways put one at my disposal on every trip. When I travelled on LLANSTEPHAN CASTLE hauling the down 'Pembroke Coast Express' from Paddington to Newport, it was a great experience to ride through the Severn Tunnel on the footplate and to clock just over '80' in the centre of it. My nephew met us at Newport station and took us to his farm up in the hills, where we had a wonderful dinner, chatted and rested in the afternoon. He then took us back to Newport, where we joined the 'South Wales Pullman' and rode on EARL OF SHAFTESBURY back to Paddington.

I felt like one in a million, riding the footplate, as one had to have a string of letters after one's name or be a colonel or a lord to get a footplate ride in those days. Every engine I travelled on was specially cleaned up for me. LLANSTEPHAN CASTLE was the cleanest Castle I ever saw and both A3s looked brand new.

I also had footplate trips on two Kings, on the up and down 'Cambrian Coast Express' between Paddington and Birmingham and on two more Merchant Navies on the up and down 'Bournemouth Belle'. Perhaps the greatest thrill of all was my last trip on the up 'Atlantic Coast Express' from Exeter to Waterloo. The only way I could get to Exeter in time was to go from Paddington and so I rode on DRUID, a Warship class diesel hydraulic, on the down 8.30am 'Royal Duchy'. It was rather like riding with the driver on a tram but it was far more interesting than sitting in the train.

I walked across Exeter and joined HOLLAND AMERICA LINE. The inspector had not arrived and though I had a permit, the driver was a bit wary at first but I soon persuaded him to take me. At that time the 'ACE' was the fastest steam train in the country, 170 miles with only one stop. The line from Exeter to Salisbury is like a corkscrew and we gained time all the way. It was a never-to-be-forgotten run, with speeds of 88 at Brookwood, 85 at Woking and 88 again at Byfleet.

My great interest and fascination with locomotive nameplates goes back to the early 1930s. The prices at which they were sold in those days might seem cheap now but they were not considered cheap then, especially in relation to the wages of the time. As an example of the latter, I well remember a friend of mine who was a shunter on the LMS, who had eight children and earned 37s 6d a week (£1.87½).

It was in January 1935 that I purchased my first nameplate, LNWR GLADIATOR for 10s (50p). Two months later I bought GWR EVENING STAR for 17s 6d (87½p). Since then I have had several hundred plates through my hands. Among them have been Southern Railway KING ARTHUR for fourteen years and QUEEN GUINEVERE for twelve years. About three or four years ago I was offered the incredible sum of £3000 for these two plates but turned it down. Since then, I understand, this man has either lost or spent all his money. However, I have recently been offered even more and I think it quite probable that I shall accept this latest offer for several reasons. Certainly, due to my great age (!), the terrible state of the country, and the fact that such an offer would be extremely unlikely ever to occur again, I must give it serious thought.

I still have my beautiful WILD DUCK, the LNWR George the Fifth 4-4-0, which will continue to adorn my oak beam for all time. Those Georges were probably the most wonderful 4-4-0s ever built. During the First World War they used to take 470 tons up the 1 in 70 of Camden bank unassisted. Twenty years later lighter trains hauled by

4-6-0s were being banked up the same incline. These 'little engines' weighed less than sixty tons and had a tractive effort of 20,000lb as against 40,000lb for a King. I still have *The Railway Magazine* for January 1912 in which there is a full account of the amazing run made by WILD DUCK. Due to the brakes seizing on while climbing Camden bank, the train came to a standstill. It was eleven minutes late passing Willesden and yet every minute had been regained by Stafford. This was with 410 tons behind the tender. Oddly enough, I recently met a man who assured me that if I would sell him WILD DUCK, he would willingly sell his house. He is not married! This plate, however, will always be here.

Right. Great Western 'King' No.6009 KING CHARLES II arriving at Birmingham Snow Hill on 4 July 1959 with the up Saturday 'Cambrian Coast Express'. Photograph Michael Mensing.

Below. The sheer range of sights on offer was such a feature of Basil Spencer's time. How about this, a Webb Coal Tank in LMS days, probably in the 1930s but where? Best guess is at East Croydon on a push-and-pull (motor-train in LNWR parlance) from Willesden Junction. This was part of the Mansion House service in LNW days.

Right. A magnificent view of new Kings at Old Oak, kindly arranged by the GW publicity men.

You'll Remember those Black and White Days...

Endpiece

You'll Remember those Black and White Days...